Healing for the Church

Healing for the Church

New Life for You and Your Church

Second, Expanded Edition

Harold Ewing Burchett

Bringing Christ Back Ministries
www.bcbministries.com

First edition 1989, published by the author
Second, expanded edition published 2015 by
Bringing Christ Back Ministries
www.bcbministries.com

ISBN: 978-0-9898179-3-6

Cover design by Barry Durham

Printed in the United States of America

The Scripture quotations in this publication are taken from the *Holy Bible: New International Version,* copyright © 1973, 1978, 1984 by the International Bible Society. Used by permission of Zondervan Bible Publishers.

Contents

Figures

Preface to the Second, Expanded Edition

God has been pleased to bless the books I have written. At their heart is the theme of the power and glory of the local church. I have therefore been eager to develop even further my presentation in Healing for the Church: New Life for You and Your Church. This second edition gives special emphasis to a plan of discipling among and between the members and is aimed at preparing each one to begin a lifetime of upbuilding others. Ultimately, this leads to the production and reproduction of leaders for the church. Furthermore, it will develop a type of church life that expresses itself in vital neighborhood segments, and exports itself to more distant locations, including other countries. A truly healthy church can expect to move from traditional isolation to biblical kinds of involvement, including expressions as house churches in all the neighborhoods where members live. The book's extensive appendixes (now expanded) are a key part of this book, giving detailed guidance in specific points mentioned in the main text.

Introduction

Struggling for exciting and permanent new life for one's church without discovering new vitality for one's own spiritual life is futile. Never the one without the other. The two go together—inseparably.

Just as believers are said to be united to Christ as a body to its head, or as a bride to her groom, so Scripture clearly teaches the profound power and glory of the universal church, a power and glory shared by each local church.

There must be no substituting of platitudes for the reality of the Spirit's power. Rather, there must be a deep hungering and searching the Scripture for what God says about his church. Merely seeking after conference programs to hear something that brings fresh excitement can never be enough.

Today we have megachurches, with attendance in the thousands, and today also we have divided, faltering churches attended by few, and in between we have all kinds of "fellowships." But how often do we find a church that is full of the power, life, and glory befitting Christ's body, with the Lord himself being its living Head? This is how Scripture describes the true church, which is made up of local assemblies, or churches. A local church's flow of life must come through its vital attachment to its Head, the Lord Jesus Christ.

Perhaps many readers have witnessed the spectacle of a church, once very strong in its preaching ministry, sinking to a low, sad state—and that very quickly after its popular preacher has moved on. Such an assembly grew large but not strong. When weight is added to an organism apart from new strength, health declines ultimately.

Picture those who for years have sat in their church hearing "sound Bible teaching" but are still unable to explain and share basic Bible truths. Perhaps their church is suffering from obesity! Somehow Satan's wiles have worked to distance these church people from Christ himself. It may take some years before any signs of trouble are evident, but if the full orb of biblical church life is not developed, difficult days are ahead. Surely, we ought not be "unaware of his [Satan's] schemes" (2 Cor. 2:11).

Churches today commonly strive for "life" and "growth" in two other ways: by the funding of Christian agencies, sometimes referred to as parachurch organizations, or by funding a larger church staff. Either way, the body of Christ is exercised in giving money but not so much in raising up its own ministering ones.

Often more deadly than this striving for a bigger church body is the stagnation widespread among those bogged in ruts of their own doing as they attempt to figure out what seems to work best. It is painful to see God's precious assembly, purchased with the blood of his Son, tied in knots with cumbersome traditions and pounded by disruptive new trends.

But more than the survival and welfare of our homeland churches is at stake. What are we exporting around the world? Missionaries who have themselves not experienced a full life in a proper biblical fellowship are unwitting carriers of spiritual infections. Can they see happen "over there" what they missed at home?

Much of the worship forms and program activities seen throughout our land today are not prescribed by Scripture. To discover their origin and roots, one must look at the theater and

2

the entertainment world. The striving to entertain and keep the audience while gaining some contributions from them is hardly based on the Bible. Furthermore, selecting and scheduling religious movies, instructional videos, book reviews, special speakers, and concert artists on the basis of their ability to draw the largest crowds does not point the way to spiritual strength.

At best a cheerful enthusiasm may exist for a time, but as with any hybrid, it cannot impel itself into the next generation. After a few soaring years, the irresistible downward draft takes all in its grip.

It must be faced—a terrible evil tide is rolling against us. As marriages and homes disintegrate at an increasing rate, the evangelical church has made perceptible adjustments in its teachings. Rather than challenging and changing our society, congregations are busying themselves learning from the world. Though the covers of a kind of "love" and "relevance" are pulled over the sores of immorality, weaknesses in many a church are apparent.

But if the church, Christ's bride, has stumbled, will she find help from us, or shall we attack and humiliate her? If one would hesitate to stone the adulterous woman whom Christ pardoned, ought not one be very hesitant to throw rocks at the Lord's own bride, for whom he died? God will stand on the side of those who love the church.

Perhaps one asks, "What can I do?" And, "If I am not certain what an ideal church would be like, how, then, could I help my church reach such a goal?"

I am persuaded that many readers can help if given better understanding of exactly what is occurring in churches and what God intends to happen. To the disheartened I would say, "Do not quit your church. Read on!"

A church functioning in God's full power and in accordance with his Word is able to cast off infections and grow. Also a continuing expansion will result because a lively local church does not dead-end in a single congregation. Viewed properly, *it is a movement*—from each individual to his or her family, from families to neighborhood expressions of church life, and continuing out to other nations.

In quest of this life, some advocate a tightly organized approach. Others emphasize great freedom to perform all sorts of "spiritual" ministries. The pastor rules all in certain communions, while other churches all but disintegrate in the trend toward subdivision into small groups. Instances of failure have marred each approach. Organization does not in itself bring power and blessing, nor does a forced disorganization.

The Scriptures, however, give important place to structure and form in the churches—for three reasons. First, the church stands as Christ's body on earth, the temple of God. We are our Lord's own bride being prepared for heaven. Second, the church's form and life are divinely designed to foster the personal holiness and corporate usefulness that God requires. Sanctification and service go together with the proper church life set forth in the Epistles. Third, successful extension of Christianity among all nations of the world issues both out of, and also into, a proper church life.

Fresh life will not come by way of a freedom from leadership and structure but through a recovery of proper biblical structure and a vital production of able leaders. Here is a basic tenet underlying proposals of this book: *Adequate leadership is both a cause and a result of a proper church life, and proper church life is both the cause and result of basic Christianity.*

Saints in disarray will never persevere in, let alone propagate, the truths God has committed to us. Furthermore, ordered church life is dependent upon the presence and continued preparation of adequate leaders. Many of the other problems to be discussed are related to this one.

Whenever a church engages members in responsibility and service without, in turn, giving those leaders the necessary edifying input, difficulties lurk somewhere ahead. Even if the church is happily going forward with its programs and adding to its membership, the seeds of death are being sown. The core of regular workers and leaders must be personally edified and also strengthened with regular additions to their ranks.

Underlying so many of the contemporary church's woes is the neglect of personal ministry to individuals. Regardless of what changes are introduced, they are only stylistic ones if basic edification and discipling of individuals is not done.

Our obsession with public ministries—to the congregation, classes, or groups—has resulted in loss of skill in discipling between individuals. Average believers are not prepared and encouraged to know and use Scripture for themselves.

Deeply hidden attitudes have tended to seal Scripture from those in the pew. Somehow the feeling exists that the Bible is the sourcebook for the sermonizer and staff teachers. The sheep lying in green pastures are, without realizing it, viewing Scripture as a sacred communication to their clergy-shepherds.

Whatever is real and essential about the church must be able to exist underground—in forests, in homes, and through war and traumatic transition. Indeed, Christ's assemblies are often seen prospering in adversity. Quite obviously, then, what may be identified on a prominent city street as "our church" must contain much more than the visible facilities and traditional things.

In fact, wherever and whenever God's people gather as his assembly, it is a unique place and time. He promises to be present specially. Therefore, let no one say that attending such gatherings does not matter. Rather than dropping or altering what God commands, we would do far better to strive with all our hearts to recover the dignity, power, and glory of the church.

Much is in print on the church and its life, often coming from learned specialists but more suited for the classroom and professional seminars. This book has no such roots or similar objectives.

What is needed today is a very ground-level (if not down-in-the-trenches) view of things, along with a strong heavenly dimension. Whether these pages meet this need, I leave to readers and their Lord to decide as they walk the paths I have laid out.

The object of this book is to help believers recover their life in Christ. As this happens, they will be able to aid their churches in discovering a vigorous corporate life. To light the way, the biblical philosophy of the church will be set forth in these chapters, along with practical instructions for its recovery and implementation.

No doubt, pastors will have special interest in the contents, but I have written rather personally to the general membership who find themselves perplexed or even disheartened. I have plotted a way out and up.

Any essential but more technical material, which might impede the movement of the writing or hamper its appeal to general readers, appears in the several appendixes. These appendixes are important, and I hope readers will invest the time necessary to study thoroughly the material presented there.

Consider the determined desire of the Hebrew exiles who grieved for their lost land. "May my tongue cling to the roof of my mouth if I do not remember you, if I do not consider Jerusalem my highest joy" (Ps. 137:6). God grant us a new desire toward the church of Christ. Remember David's burning zeal as he was house-hunting for God: "I will not enter my house or go to my bed—I will allow no sleep to my eyes, no slumber to my eyelids, till I find a place for the LORD, a dwelling for the Mighty One of Jacob" (Ps. 132:3-5). The Christian congregations are now God's dwelling place. Has our zeal faded and vision dimmed?

All that David dreamed of was finally destroyed. With face awash with bitter tears, the prophet Jeremiah gave this solemn interpretation of the tragedy: "The kings of the earth did not believe, nor did any of the world's people, that enemies and foes could enter the gates of Jerusalem. But it happened because of the sins of her prophets and the iniquities of her priests, who shed within her the blood of the righteous" (Lam. 4:12-13).

Today we find ourselves stumbling but not yet fallen. There are deep wounds, disillusionment, and divisions, compounded by a deadening ignorance.

But God is being gracious and longsuffering toward us. We can discover and experience the full life of glory intended for the church of Christ. So we take new hope and lay out plans for a return to God and his way of doing things. Then to him will be "glory in the church and in Christ Jesus throughout all generations, for ever and ever! Amen" (Eph. 3:21).

1

A Troubling Look

And the two will become one. . . . I am talking about Christ
and the church.

—Eph. 5:31-32

Picture a thriving family expanding into a veritable living
movement. That is what a church is supposed to be. God says
so. Each church must be prepared to produce other churches by
dividing itself as a living cell, and also by sending church planters
to more distant areas.

Soon we shall delight ourselves in viewing the blessings
intended for the church. But for now ours is a more sobering
chore. We must survey things as they are. The church scene is
disturbing.

As we start our trek together, let us make our footing sure
by ridding ourselves of all doubt. The fearful stumble easily.
It should never enter our minds that what God expects from
his children cannot be accomplished. He expects the church to
thrive. It can. Your church can become alive and fruitful for God.

Cries of confusion today are many and loud. "Let's get better
organized!" is heard on the one hand. On the other hand, many
argue for less organization in the church. However, the solution
to our problems does not lie in either direction. The new surge of

life needed by the church will come neither through complicating the organization nor through simplifying it.

We need to ask and answer the simplest and most basic of questions: Who are we? Where are we going? How shall we get there? These must be understood clearly by leaders and members alike.

Asking the Pastors

Here are three questions I sometimes have asked pastors in unsigned surveys:

1. What is your church supposed to be doing?
2. How is this to be done—by what means?
3. How do you evaluate your progress toward your goals?

Now please remember, as you look at typical answers collected from one group of evangelical leaders, that they were instructed—even urged—to be specific and not resort to generalities about "evangelizing the lost and edifying the saints." Here are some of the answers:

1. What is your church supposed to be doing?
    *   Win souls to Christ and help our town.
    *   Preach and teach the gospel and win others.
    *   Reach out to the unsaved and help the saved.
    *   Join in fellowship with believers.
2. How is this to be done—by what means?
    *   We should really love the Lord and know the Word.
    *   Preaching, teaching, living a life of example.
    *   Personal contact—visitation and getting to know people in our area.
    *   Reach souls for Christ, feed the believers.

3. How do you evaluate your progress toward your goals?
    *   Not so hot.
    *   [No answer given.]
    *   Not very well. Poor.
    *   Trying to have more visitation among believers and unsaved.

A kind of benumbing confusion has us in its grip. On the one side of the confusion is complacency. At the opposite extreme is a contrived effort toward charisma. But do not go sour on what God has revealed as his way of doing things. He is the one who says, "I will build my church, and the gates of Hades will not overcome it" (Matt. 16:18).

Many have put the ax of overreaction to their traditions, but that approach in itself will not produce new life. Others are halting between options of wildfire or no fire. Ample glory and power is available to God's people when they properly align themselves with the Head.

Looking into the streets of society to discover the latest happenings and thus be relevant is not the way either. Pitiful are the insecure saints who plead to be recognized as somewhat like everyone else. We do not need these sad peeps of "Me too!" God's prophets, priests, and princes must do better than that! "You will know how people ought to conduct themselves in God's household, which is the church of the living God, the pillar and foundation of the truth" (1 Tim. 3:15). Notice the certainty and grandness of the church in Paul's view. This is why all of Satan's forces must not and may not conquer.

Our Savior is positioned among the golden lampstands in Revelation 1, indicating he is present with the churches. Then, reading in chapters 2 and 3 of the weaknesses of those assemblies, one suspects they would be cast off by people today in rash, premature judgment. It is dangerous, though, to put out a light that God is protecting.

One other text we might examine at this point is Ephesians 2:19-22: "Consequently, you are no longer foreigners and aliens, but fellow citizens with God's people and members of God's household, built on the foundation of the apostles and prophets, with Christ Jesus himself as the chief cornerstone. In him the whole building is joined together and rises to become a holy temple in the Lord. And in him you too are being built together to become a dwelling in which God lives by his Spirit."

Even a surface study of this text will show serious divine planning in the makeup and life of the church. And this one universal church is expressed in local assemblies. The structure, fellowship, and activities of your church, then, are not matters God has left to our own choosing. These are determined by him.

However, wide and even contradictory differences exist between many church groups today. What are we to make of this?

How Do We Decide Who Is Right?
On every hand we see radical differences between churches—even among churches of the same denomination. Let me warn that this investigation can be very discouraging. First of all, we have the spectacle of many fundamentalists and evangelicals who energetically stand for the reliability and authority of God's Word when it deals with redemption but who ignore the sections dealing with the church.

Still more puzzling is the fact that many differing churches seek to prove their unique positions from the very same Scriptures. Since the Bible does not contradict itself, these major differences must arise because the Word is not being used fairly. Here is a simple plan for looking at the New Testament that will help in deciding between differing views about the church.

| 5 Books of History | ◄——————— | 22 Books of Commentary |

There are twenty-seven books in the New Testament, and this simple diagram indicates that the first five books, which are history, are to be interpreted by the remaining twenty-two books that make up the testament. Matthew, Mark, Luke, John, and Acts tell the story and show the various activities of our Lord and the apostles. While it is true that much basic teaching is given in the parables, sermons, and recorded experiences, it is also true that we may not safely ignore God's own interpretations, which follow in the remainder of the New Testament. For example, it is improper for one to point to a happening in the narrative section of the New Testament and make that activity obligatory for our day. Even if Jesus is shown spending much time on the open road walking from town to town in sandals, that does not mean that each faithful minister must do the same!

When God expects us to make something in the first five books our literal, permanent model, it will be clear enough in the instructions and church practice delineated in the final twenty-two books. The Epistles are given for that very purpose of enlightenment. Here, then, are three safe standards for interpreting Scripture on this vital subject of the church:

1. *Each* basic essential for church life is revealed in Scripture.
2. *Nothing* may be made basic and essential unless it is revealed in the Scripture as being basic and essential.
3. *Everything* revealed as basic and essential must be treated as such with full obedience.

Two further observations need to be made. First, it is

impossible to argue conclusively from the Bible's silence on any subject. Trying to establish or condemn a teaching or practice on the basis of what Scripture does *not* say is quite unsound.

Second, a principle of flexibility must be employed when considering church structure. Even in Bible days the assemblies were not all exactly alike. Considerable freedom in the worship and organization was present. Yet, I take it that the three standards mentioned in connection with the diagram above were surely followed as the young churches developed. The Epistles gave them special guidance.

What, Then, Is a Church?

All who are truly Christ's are said in Scripture to be members of his body. Thus, the Lord is the divine Head of the church, and his body is expressed on earth in the form of local assemblies. The Bible is definite enough in revealing the structure and nature of church life. It is a costly mistake to set aside this portion of God's revelation.

Life in a local church should flow along lines that agree with biblical principles. Orders should come down from the headquarters of heaven. Church programs and goals ought not to evolve merely from circumstances or styles of the day. Scriptural principles should prevail over any contrary, even long-standing, tradition or more modern fashion and pressing circumstances.

The church, then, is a living organism joined to its divine Head, under his control. Just as the body is a vehicle for expressing one's spirit, so the church functions on our Lord's behalf.

Furthermore, a true body of Christ must have, and does have, capacities for growing and reproducing other bodies of believers like itself. It is indeed unfortunate if the very program and pace of schedule of a church tend to negate rather than forward God's purposes for it.

Do We Want More, Like We Are?

A neighboring pastor once invited me to conduct evangelistic services at his church. He went on to explain, "We are small—only about 65 members."

"How many of your members have personally led another person to the Savior?" I asked.

"That is our big problem, and that is precisely why we need you to come and lead the crusade."

"But let us suppose that during our crusade your attendance doubled. You would then have 130 members who would tend to be like one another. What would be the significance of our effort? Are you sure you want more of what you already have?" Arrangements with me for the crusade were dropped at that point.

What is the real core problem? Whatever it is, it will obviously lie at the heart of the entire subject of this writing. Let me here present a little equation for our help:

Non-Soul-Winning Church + ? = Soul-Winning Church

What missing ingredient must a non-soul-winning church add to itself to equal a soul-winning church?

Surely evangelistic training alone is not the answer. As soon as the program pressure is removed, the people cease to function. Numbers who have earned diplomas in personal evangelism courses still do not witness.

This failure rises from a defect in spiritual nourishment. Such churches are not properly edified. Members have not been discipled into true spiritual life and are not discipling one another.

What, then, can alter a church and make it truly vital and reproducing? The answer is *edification*—that wholesome flow of spiritual truth from the Head to the body, as it is shared between members. How powerful this is will become much clearer as we proceed. First, however, we must peer even deeper into the darkness that is choking contemporary churches.

2

Something Is Drastically Wrong—
Beginning the Diagnosis

My tears have been my food day and night,
while men say to me all day long, "Where is your God?"
—Ps. 42:3

Most adults today have witnessed the spectacle of churches divided and defeated by confusion and sin. Or perhaps they have seen a group shriveled, struggling, almost lifeless, and yet clinging to a schedule of activities. But I wish to focus briefly on the "strong" and "vibrant" churches. One of this type I once led in what turned out to be a most silent meeting.

That period of shocked quiet came about when I asked how many individuals the entire congregation had brought to Christ. About one hundred persons were present at the prayer service where this took place. Not one reply could I get from them.

Finally, I called to the deacon seated in the front row. "Would you say that together the members perhaps have led five to Christ?" (I had already made it clear that I was not referring to decisions made as a result of the church services or programs within the walls of the buildings; rather, I was referring to their ineffective witness to the outside community.)

"If you want to be generous, then let's say five," he finally

16

responded, shaking his head, eyes cast downward in a display of shame. Then I invited him to step to the blackboard at the front. Addressing the assembly, I asked how many had been believers from between 40 and 50 years. Four hands were raised. This number had held to faith in Christ on an average of 45 years each, I figured, so I instructed the good deacon to multiply 4 × 45 and write the total number of years on the board.

Next I asked all those who had lived in the faith from between 30 and 40 years to raise their hands. A larger group responded. Then the deacon multiplied that number of persons times the average of 35 years and put the total on the board.

An even larger number indicated they had believed in Christ from between 20 and 30 years. Their total years also was listed. This procedure was continued until we had also included the several who were converted during the past year.

All were counted and the grand total written at the bottom of the list. It added to 1,013 years (a number I shall never forget!), and I made a poignant, though admittedly rather biting, observation: "In a little more than 1,000 years of combined effort, we have reached five souls. If our Lord does not return first and we are able to invest another millennium of effort, we shall have ten. What a revival!" That is when the silence came. No one moved or spoke for a long while. You could hear yourself breathe.

Another church, counted as highly successful, takes in more new members in a single year than make up their entire Wednesday night prayer service attendance. Something is wrong there. Not growing and maybe dying is their condition.

For some years I have been asking pastors, active church leaders, and students what conception they have of their church. They are asked to make an outline of the church program. Usually the papers come in with a list of familiar institutions something

17

like this:

1. Public services
2. Sunday School
3. Small groups
4. Missions
5. Administration

This view of the church may be common, but it is inadequate, if not fatal. What the Bible does not mention as essential is given the main emphasis. Perhaps a diagram will help.

NOT THIS: <u>**Institutions**</u>   **BUT THIS:** <u>**Ministries**</u>

Ministries ↗   *Institutions* ↗

Let me explain the above illustration. We must subordinate our traditional institutions to those ministries clearly defined in Scripture. Thus, when God says in the Bible that believers ought to build up one another and to extend the church through evangelism, then those ministries (discipling and evangelism) are to be our main objectives. Any program raised up should be aimed at carrying out the biblically assigned objectives.

For example, the Sunday School is a fine institution—especially when there is serious Bible teaching and effort to deal with the hearts of people. However, it is a mistake to conceive of teaching and evangelizing as only a means of building up the Sunday School. It must be the other way around. Our Sunday Schools, if they are to exist, must do so in order to carry out God's mandates of edification and evangelism.

The trouble is, we have made our services, activities, and organizations the grand end. And the sacred ministries that God makes essential are now viewed simply as the means to build up and sustain our institutions.

Many of our organizations and activities today are not so much as named in the Bible. That fact, however, does not make them bad—not if they can be used to carry on the God-ordained ministries assigned to us in Scripture.

Our individual lives and the total programs and life of the church must be subordinated to what God makes essential. Those programs that forward the great ministries of the Spirit are good. Others may be a hindrance. None must occupy positions as grand goals for church life. Our traditions and institutions, if they are to be blessed of God, must prove themselves as legitimate, effective means toward divine ends. And we know from Scripture what the ends are to be.

Youth ministry, Sunday School, or missionary programs are not the urgent causes for which the church exists. Rather, these ministries and programs are the means of accomplishing God's assigned tasks. Once viewed wrongly as a "great cause" for which we are to give our life and funds, the program is institutionalized and tends to elevate itself as a special end. Ultimately the church will be viewed as subordinate to the claims of its institutions.

Perhaps large questions loom before the mind at this point. How does one get from where we are now to where we should be? What can a pastor do against a tide of faulty tradition? Or still more daunting, what if I am not a top leader in my church— what can I do?

There is something you can do. But you must have the basic principles of church life fixed definitely in your mind. And you will need a plan of fostering that kind of life from your own vantage point.

Our next chapter will focus on moving toward a vital church fellowship. This may require some change in structure so as to make the local church more biblical and also strong enough to affect and stir today's society.

Later we will see how to make church meetings alive and edifying. Then we will see how to get daily teaching out into the home, and finally how to spread the life of the church throughout the community and into other nations. Underlying all of this will be a specific plan for stimulating individual edification among members of the local church.

3

Changing a Church

Why are you downcast, O my soul?
   Why so disturbed within me?
Put your hope in God,
   for I will yet praise him,
   my Savior and my God.
                              —Ps. 42:5

God is near the one who helps the church change. But what can change a church? *A full-orbed plan of edification can meet the challenge.* This chapter is dedicated to ideas calculated to move an assembly of believers toward a new relationship with God and one another. Keep in mind two basic considerations:

1. The great functional purposes of the church must be observed:
    a.. Edification
    b.. Evangelism
2. The structure of the church must be right.

Before looking at the proper offices and structure of the church, let us concern ourselves with the two main functions or ministries of the church—its upbuilding and its extension.

First, the edification of any church should take place both in public and also in the private, personal dimensions. In each of these dimensions there must be a planned, regular ministry, as well as the more spontaneous sharing of truth.

This means that four kinds of edification will be taking place in an alive assembly. Count them: Publicly, there will be prepared sermons, as well as the more spontaneous testimonies, each in their appropriate place. Then, individual members will be engaged in discipling one another. Not only this, but they must know how to counsel and build up one another quite spontaneously as needs arise—whether on the telephone, at the back of the church, or perhaps talking by appointment with a distressed brother or sister.

A major thesis of this book concerns the integral relationships between edification and evangelism. Why do not Christians witness and evangelize as they should? It is not simply that they lack training in evangelism. Many have had such training and still do not evangelize. Stunted, immature people populate numbers of fiery evangelistic churches. The explanation is clear. Evangelism does not provide for edification, but a proper edification always provides for evangelism. No believer has been properly discipled and taught who is not concerned with reproduction.

Still further, the term "reproduction" means more than helping to birth other believers. Reproduction must include bringing others of the body to find and fill their places of ministry. I would even go so far as to say that no pastor knows his assignment as he ought until he is able to teach another how to do what he does.

Half-Awakenings

Any spiritual awakening not accompanied by corrective teaching on church life is only partial and temporary. Surely Christ's stated purpose to present his bride "as a radiant church, without stain or wrinkle or any other blemish" will include changes in petrified official structures and programs.

Strong cries are heard today for something relevant, contemporary, and effective. However, nothing is so relevant and in touch with the world as *people*, and a church is made up of people—a cross section of real people. People touching people is God's way.

Sometimes the problem lies in the attitudes of believers. An individualistic, independent spirit may be quite contemporary, but it is also very wrong when found within the church. Scripture does not allow us to follow our own understanding and desires in serving the Lord.

The focal point of spiritual life therefore must not shift from churches to the many Christian agencies, sometimes referred to as parachurch organizations. True, these agencies usually present themselves as arms of the church, but all too often the arms seem rather detached from local churches. They do not belong to churches, nor can any church direct their motions. Rather, such organizations are under independent boards. The question is not whether they should exist or not, but where is the nerve center to be?

Role of the Pastor Clarified

Experience shows that if a church is to change and find new life, the pastoral function should be set in order first. A study of figure 1—a three-dimensional view of a church—will provide perspective.

Allow an open, unmarked circle to represent an entire body of believers. In one sense, there is no distinction between them. (See Gal. 3:26-28.) All are in the one body and have the general commission to edify one another. The vertical lines indicate differing ministries carried out by those with the various spiritual gifts. The Holy Spirit enables them thus to function.

Figure 1: The Three Dimensions of a Church

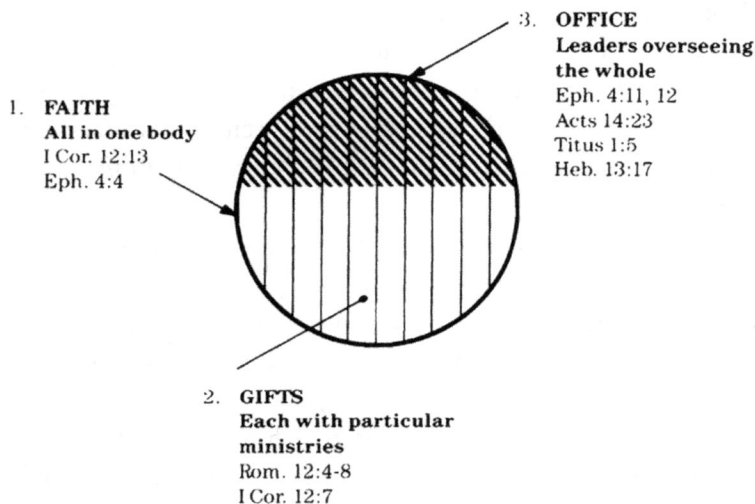

3. **OFFICE**
Leaders overseeing
the whole
Eph. 4:11, 12
Acts 14:23
Titus 1:5
Heb. 13:17

1. **FAITH**
All in one body
I Cor. 12:13
Eph. 4:4

2. **GIFTS**
Each with particular
ministries
Rom. 12:4-8
I Cor. 12:7

These gifts are listed in greatest length in Romans 12 and 1 Corinthians 12.

The overhanging shaded area is intended to suggest the church's spiritual leadership. Now let us focus upon this for a moment. Notice these leaders are first of all within the larger circle. They must, of course, be true believers in our Lord. Second, they themselves will have some of the gifts, just as any other believer does. But their distinctive service for Christ will be that of leadership. Thus, the three responsibilities of a pastor, elder, or spiritual leader in the church might be stated in the following manner:

1. Like all others, pastors share the general responsibility to love, serve, and edify fellow believers and bear witness for Christ in the outside community.

2. Like all other believers, they have their own personal ministry in the body, using their gifts in the area of shepherding people's souls, or pastoring.
3. Unlike the others, these leaders of the church are there to coordinate the activities of the whole and to direct other believers into their ministries.

If the believers throughout the church are properly pastored, they will be led to employ their gifts to the full in the complete scheme of ministries prescribed for the church. It must be added also that one who is a senior leader will have the responsibility of reproducing other leaders – raising up, if possible, other pastors. Only in this way can a church's life go full-cycle and have continuity and permanence.

The very tight and exclusive one-man pastoral rule over a church, commonly seen today, is hardly to be discovered in Scripture. Note, for example, in Acts 20:17 that "Paul sent to Ephesus for the elders of the church." Notice there is one church but a company of elders. He proceeds to exhort them: "Keep watch over yourselves and all the flock of which the Holy Spirit has made you overseers. Be shepherds of the church of God, which he bought with his own blood. I know that after I leave, savage wolves will come in among you and will not spare the flock. Even from your own number men will arise and distort the truth in order to draw away disciples after them" (vv. 28-30).

These verses make it clear that more than one or two elders made up this company. We see the plurality of the eldership again in Acts 14:23, where "Paul and Barnabas appointed elders for them in each church." See also Titus 1:5.

See appendix 1 for perspective on the common and very disastrous clergy-laity division. Today's clergy-laity distinctions are not found anywhere in Scripture.

25

It must be made very clear that, when I speak of pastoring, I am referring to the spiritual shepherding of God's people, not to church administration or to preaching and teaching. In most churches today the pastor is, of course, chief administrator and preacher. The biblical pastor might perform these duties, but not necessarily.

Not all pastors are capable public preachers, and not all preachers are capable pastors. These two functions require differing spiritual abilities. God does not always place both these capacities in the same individual. Often, yes, but not always. Distinguishing between these gifts is wholesome and realistic.

A Growing Plan of Shepherding the Church

Early in the process of upturn in a church's life should come a growing plan of shepherding. Men must be trained and prepared to join the shepherding team, and the church must be prepared to receive them in their shepherding ministries.

Too often churches who enlist leaders to help in spiritual oversight of the congregation begin with too large a number. Consequently, discouragement sets in as defaults and failures multiply. Perhaps it could be stated as a rule that the broader the recruitment of shepherds, the more general and less seriously the pastoral responsibilities will be taken.

Time must be invested in challenging the leaders concerning the urgent need for multiplying shepherds in the church. The seriousness of the calling must be made very real before any are designated as additions to the pastoral team.

Beginning with two or three who really are committed is better than struggling with a larger number who have not the vision and calling. Shepherding must be uppermost with them, and it will mean a change of life and schedule.

Serious training sessions will be needed to prepare the men.

Soon the Spirit of God will begin to show what fine work can be performed by shepherds from the ranks of the church. Here is a list of ministries I have seen carried out by shepherds:

1. Recover delinquents (see chap. 5 for a more complete discussion of discipline and recovery of backsliders).
2. Increase fellowship among families in each shepherding area.
3. Arrange for home prayer meetings.
4. Establish prayer chains.
5. Lead family training in each residential section.
6. Care for ill and shut-ins through visitation, share tape-recorded services from church, arrange for Communion.
7. Give oversight to incoming new members.
8. Counsel troubled and ill people.
9. Make special effort to develop other leaders, not simply do one's own duties.
10. Develop the master plan of the local church as a congregation of neighborhood fellowships led by leaders who shepherd families in each residential section where members of the congregation reside.

Another very important function of the shepherd is that of going into homes and helping parents shepherd their children. At the outset of such a visit, the shepherd must make sure that each parent is a true believer in Christ. Next, the shepherd will inquire about the spiritual life of each household member.

Also help can be offered the family members in evangelizing their neighbors and friends. An attractive piece of gospel literature can be provided each one, along with practical hints in personal evangelism. Where advisable, a home evangelistic study should be started.

"How is family worship coming along?" is a definite inquiry that should be made. If the home altar has fallen, the shepherd should be prepared then and there to have a meaningful time of spiritual sharing and worship involving the whole family. They will need simple directions about carrying this on regularly.

These helpful home visits with the entire family present offer opportunities to discover and upgrade the doctrinal understanding of the members. A brief series of questions followed by simple instructions would be profitable. The visit also affords an opportunity to find out what possible ministries are of most interest to those being interviewed.

It is evident that such a plan will require discipline and economy in time. If the shepherd is to succeed, he will need to exercise discretion and a sober, earnest spirituality. He may not simply relax and enjoy himself but must make each minute count, limiting a visit to about one hour. If both the leaders and the church body are fully prepared, each family will look forward to such a visit, and the effort will stir the congregation very deeply.

A More-Definite Structure

Notice the leaders mentioned in Ephesians 4:11: "It was [Christ] who gave some to be apostles, some to be prophets, some to be evangelists, and some to be pastors and teachers." Roughly, the first three gifted ones mentioned are concerned with the expansion and establishment of new churches, whereas the functions of pastoring and teaching are directed at caring for and building up already-planted churches. From the apostles themselves we learn that their office was limited and special. We see this in the care they showed in replacing Judas, and also in Paul's defense of his credentials as a true apostle. Today, any continuing responsibility to pioneer, plant, and establish churches belongs to the missionary-evangelist.

In appendix 2 on spiritual gifts, it will be seen that the prophetic function has been much affected by God's giving us the New Testament Scripture. Now, the preacher who expounds these sacred writings fulfills a prophetic function.

As Scripture unfolds God's permanent plan for the church, we find that a leader of the local church is called elder, bishop (or overseer), and pastor (or shepherd). The terms are used more or less interchangeably in the Bible, as a careful study of Scripture will prove. See Acts 20:17, 28; Philippians 1:1; 1 Timothy 3:1-7; 5:17; Titus 1:5-9; 1 Peter 5:1-2.

After a couple of centuries had passed, the meaning of elder, bishop, pastor had become altered in people's thinking, and each term was made very distinct from the other. However, if we return to the original biblical content of the titles, we see that "elder" was a term growing out of ancient synagogue usage and signified the rank and dignity of the office. In contrast, "bishop" and "pastor" were intended to emphasize the duty of overseeing or pastoring God's flock.

Many Christian communities today agree that elder and deacon are the two biblical offices. However, the concepts of bishop-overseer and pastor-shepherd are often improperly distinguished and even removed from the local church eldership.

For those who have further interest in developing a biblical eldership, the listing in appendix 3 could prove helpful.

Encouraging Spiritual Capabilities

When the structure of the church becomes more sound and biblical—especially in the pastoral areas—spiritual gifts are next in order of concern. Appendix 2 addresses this matter at length.

It needs to be said, however, that a church's organization and program should move along biblical lines and thus involve each member in ministry of some kind. All believers have been endowed with particular gifts from God for service. A few will fill offices, but all should serve. "Now to each one the manifestation of the Spirit is given for the common good" (1 Cor. 12:7).

In order for this powerful pattern of life to be realized in an assembly of believers, effort must be put forth. Regular teaching on the Holy Spirit's work in equipping the church will be essential. Many will require practical assistance in discovering their particular gifts. All will need definite training in effective ministry.

The Church's Prayer Life

Because of its primary importance, the matter of deep, significant prayer in the life of the church should not be placed chronologically down the line but should run concurrently with all steps of progress. The secret of all spiritual accomplishment lies here—in the "greater things" promised by Jesus:

> I tell you the truth, anyone who has faith in me will do what I have been doing. He will do even greater things than these, because I am going to the Father. And I will do whatever you ask in my name, so that the Son may bring glory to the Father. You may ask me for anything in my name, and I will do it. (John 14:12-14)

Prayer is spiritual breathing. It takes more out of you to hold your breath than to breathe. In fact, breathing adds life—you were designed to breathe. Just so, prayer should be normal. Many Christians, blue in the face, wonder why life's race is difficult. By prayer, we can get far beyond our self-interests.

Responsible believers, wishing to see their church awakened to a new life of prayer, would do well to follow these steps:

1. Set in order your own prayer life and, if married, that of your spouse and that of your whole family.

2. Train other individuals to pray. People in general are ignorant regarding prayer and also neglectful and ineffectual. Show them how to worship God using Bible texts that describe him or his works. Other truths and promises are to be read and claimed in prayer. Even a few praying ones will spread new life into church meetings.

3. Train prayer group leaders thoroughly. This includes any who preside over groups at church or in home meetings that might exist for prayer.

4. Work with key leaders, enlisting them to help enliven and keep on course any prayer meetings they attend, always being ready to participate.

5. Encourage stronger prayer emphasis in regular church services, involving the congregation in prayers of worship, thanksgiving, and petition. This can be done both by selection of individuals to share in the order of worship and by inviting spontaneous participation. However, the focus must be on training and preparing people to approach God in prayer.

6. Stimulate and deepen the weekly prayer service. Make it the chief item on the weekday calendar.

7. Hold days of prayer. This should be done periodically by individuals as well as by the church family. Appendix 4 gives practical suggestions for conducting both private and public days of prayer.

8. Gather families in the various residential areas and offer serious practical training in the conduct of family worship.

9. Encourage children to participate in public prayer.

10. Develop special intercessory groups for men, women, and young people.

11. Give prayer a larger place in all official meetings, such as that of committees and staff. Never begin a session with an

insipid "word of prayer." Consider every prayer a meeting with God. Demonstrate to God and man how very much divine guidance is needed.

Principles to Keep in Mind while Making Changes

1. Very real, steady growth will follow the real, steady investment of proper effort.

2. Right attitudes and wrong methods are generally to be preferred above right methods and wrong attitudes.

3. Never back into a position. (Your posture or stand on important matters must be positively motivated, or you might be repulsed into extremes.)

4. Knock against nothing legitimate until you have something better already going—then still do not knock.

5. Similarly, never discard something good for something better until that better thing is functioning.

6. It is generally not good to change labels (of various programs or structures) until you have changed the content.

7. Some friction is inevitable, but expressing appreciation for people of former days and older methods will ease much of the tension. Do not consider things of the past as necessarily evil.

8. Avoid frightening, agitating, driving, or forcing. Lead with life.

9. Let the dead bury the dead. Involve the more vital ones in spiritual functions.

10. New growth in love will make it easier to implement organizational changes, but mere program and organizational changes will not in themselves bring new life.

11. Watch carefully so that you do not trip over your own new insights.

4

View of a Body Functioning with Spiritual Vitality

The whole body, supported and held together by its ligaments and sinews, grows as God causes it to grow.

—Col. 2:19

When new life comes to a church, encouraging evidences will be present:

1. Church meetings alive, happy, and filled with power
2. Members edifying one another
3. Daily Bible teaching and prayer in the families
4. Thriving prayer meetings
5. Recovery of backsliders
6. Growing concern and ministry to community and world.

How the Head and Body Relate—Who Rules?
If the Lord Jesus Christ as Head of the church rules his body, members will then be unanimous at each point. Such a thought quickly raises several questions. How does a church know God's will on each occasion? How is the entire assembly to be brought under his sway? And what about those individuals who cannot or will not agree?

Perhaps the way to begin is by reassuring ourselves of God's serious devotion to the church. In Ephesians 2:19-22 believers are said to be "members of God's household," "a holy temple in the Lord," and "a dwelling in which God lives by his Spirit."

Our Lord's own love for his bride is beautifully expressed in the fifth chapter of Ephesians in such words as "Christ loved the church and gave himself up for her" (v. 25). Next we are informed that this ultimate sacrifice by our Lord is very purposeful: "to present her to himself as a radiant church, without stain or wrinkle or any other blemish, but holy and blameless" (v. 27). Thus our Lord will cooperate fully in gaining control of his body. If you long for that, he desires it even more. We are speaking about "the church of God, which he bought with his own blood" (Acts 20:28). Church life, then, is really the ongoing ministry of Christ carried out by the Holy Spirit through the body of believers.

Matthew 18:18-20 describes this operation. A disciplinary difficulty is here set forth by Jesus wherein the church is called on to make the decision. Our Lord then proceeds to explain the great authority the church has when believers are gathered together (v. 18). Next, instructions are given as to how the Lord's authority in heaven is to be exercised by us on earth. This is to be done through prayer agreement (v. 19). The following verse explains why there is such authority in united prayer. Christ is in the midst of gathered believers by means of the Holy Spirit, who indwells God's temple.

All this has very large, important implications regarding the government of a local church. It is Christ's church. He cares. He desires very much for us to know the will of God at each critical point.

The aim of all believers must therefore not be to get their own way or even to agree with others. Rather, they must seek and find the will of the Head—to agree with that will and to carry it out. All must come to the place of wholehearted subjection to the Lord of the church as his will is disclosed to his body.

Two large hindrances to Christ's rule over his people are passivity and selfishness. Finding God's will in a matter may not be left to any one person or to a select few or even to the majority. Each member of Christ's body is expected to be active and responsible in both service and decision-making. "Not my will, Lord, but thine!" must be our prayer. We are to place Christ in his place and to take our position of authority in him. Come often to these truths: "And God placed all things under his feet and appointed him to be head over everything for the church" (Eph. 1:22); "And God raised us up with Christ and seated us with him in the heavenly realms in Christ Jesus" (Eph. 2:6).

Given its place, prayer will bring the Spirit's presence. The Spirit will then unify, motivate, direct. It must be remembered that group prayer is unique and distinct from private prayer. Both are important, but there is a special manifestation of the church's Head when members of his body are met together in spiritual agreement.

How does the Head make known his will to the church as they meet to pray and consider a matter? Here are procedural steps:

1. Have the facts presented.
2. Study principles of the Word that might bear on the subject at hand. (The Holy Spirit will never lead contrary to Scripture.)
3. Pray, seeking application of the principles to the situation at hand.
4. Recognition of the Lord's will is achieved by the group.

How can this decision be unanimous, particularly when some may disagree with the conclusion of the majority? What should happen then? Through the minority, however, the Head might well be saying, "Wait!" It is important at this point to have any dissenting feelings and related information brought into the light. This is done through congregational discussions and by making personal approach to the dissenting individuals during the period of time (days, weeks, or more) set aside for further reflection and prayer.

Each seriously dissenting person must be given a full hearing in private by the leaders. It might well be discovered that they have some good insights that have not yet gotten into the mix of things. At any rate, they will appreciate the regard shown them. Antagonism will be diffused, and the feeling of being embarrassed and ignored will be avoided. All this requires patience and love, but in the long run it will be worth the effort.

What about the obstinate individual or individuals who finally refuse to offer edifying insights regarding their contrary points of view? They will by their spirit show that they are not acting under guidance of the Holy Spirit—at least not in this matter. Consequently, their dissent must be disregarded.

Only after prayer and patient waiting should any opinions be disregarded. But if it is properly done, the body may still feel that there is a unanimity among all who are in a sincere, spiritual state. It will not be necessary to allow the dissenters to rule and ruin the Spirit's guidance. Again, the Head will rule and not the majority.

In the light of these insights, let us now consider the implications of a divided body opinion. Such a split will mean one of three things:

1. Lack of understanding regarding spiritual procedure itself

36

or concerning issues at hand. Continue to pray, confer, and investigate.

2. The time is not right. Delay the matter.
3. The dissenters are not, on this issue, acting under the Spirit's guidance as a contributing member of the body. Proceed.

The procedure outlined earlier ought to be used in selection of officers, in the conduct of board and committee business, and in the larger church actions. Strive for an attitude that is not overly perfectionistic, allowing love its full latitude while necessary control is exercised and confrontations are made.

The congregation must not be sluggardly and unholy. Furthermore, there need be no dread of man or feeling that the same persons must always occupy the same positions of responsibility.

If the body remains humble, prayerful, and unrushed, successful business can be accomplished. Growth will occur. Such spiritual procedure as we are discussing trains the assembly to look to and submit to the Head, to love and regard one another, and to avoid impetuous, ill-advised action.

How the Leaders and the Congregation Relate

The elders, or spiritual leaders, must make some decisions on the body's behalf. Scripture is plain enough when it says these leaders are to "take care of God's church" (1 Tim. 3:5). Furthermore, they are to "direct the affairs of the church"; if this is done effectively, they are thus declared "worthy of double honor" (1 Tim. 5:17). Believers are to "hold them in the highest regard in love because of their work" (1 Thess. 5:13). Again Scripture orders, "Obey your leaders and submit to their authority" (Heb. 13:17).

When believers in Antioch wished to aid famine victims in

Judea, they did so by "sending their gift to the elders by Barnabas and Saul" (Acts 11:30). A search through Acts 15 will show the elders at Jerusalem sharing ultimate responsibility with the apostles.

It can be stated this way: The Head rules, and this rule is often expressed through the elders, or chief leaders and spiritual fathers, of the church. When understood and practiced correctly, the congregation will not be resentful or feel left out of things because (1) they participated in the selection and commissioning of their leaders, and (2) the full membership is given all vital, necessary information as they meet for prayer. Many issues, of course, are decided corporately in prayer.

In addition, the congregation is invited to make their opinions known to the leaders. If the times of public prayer and consultation do not seem conclusive enough, the congregation might be polled in order to determine their thinking. In no case, however, should such a sampling of the body's mind be thought of as an election or a vote on an issue. (Churches bound by a constitution and bylaws that prescribe procedures for election and voting can of course still fulfill this formality after they have proceeded as we have described. Further instructions concerning elections and installing of officers are given in appendix 5.)

Where church government requires congregational decisions on each detail of business, there need be no abrupt attack on the procedure. If there is a spirit of love and regard for the leadership, officials can function in a scriptural manner, and the congregation can render their approval in the proper, legally required fashion. As growth and insight occur, desired procedural changes can be made.

More important than exact procedure is the attitude existing between the congregation and its leaders. Members who have a right view of spiritual authority will happily appeal to their leaders for support and guidance. Officers serve the body by leading.

When the atmosphere is as it should be, committees and indeed the entire church fellowship will feel strong inclination to keep their elders posted on committee activities, group functions, or singular adventures in ministry. Individuals assuming responsibility for Christ will quite naturally request their leaders' prayer and guidance. That is the way a healthy family operates. Conflicting ventures will in this way be avoided. And standards of scheduling and coordinating activities will thus be possible.

Where the Spirit is in control, there will be a symmetry and pattern of unity in all functions and ministries as they are undertaken. One individual occasionally meeting with another would require no report to the leaders or any need for special scheduling. If, however, two individuals were to begin regular discipling sessions together, it would be fitting that this be officially noted.

Furthermore, if a group is to have a one-time gathering, it is good for this to be reported for prayer and proper scheduling. Finally, if a group is to meet regularly, this should come before the leaders in advance for their prayerful consideration, approval, and proper scheduling. These standards should be made known to the church.

As to the pastoral functions, the congregation should be taught and encouraged to hold a wholesome regard for their shepherds so that the entire pastoral team can function effectively in each emergency or situation of need. Where a spiritual awakening is in progress, needy members will more normally welcome attentive ministry from fellow members gifted in pastoral functions.

How the Members Relate to One Another

Earlier we considered this verse: "Now to each one the manifestation of the Spirit is given for the common good" (1 Cor. 12:7). Extensive treatment of this text and subject matter is given in an early chapter of my book *People Helping People*. For the moment, however, notice that the Scripture makes it clear that God equips each believer. This capability for ministry is given as a manifestation of the Holy Spirit and for the profit of all others.

So we see that God does not limit himself to working with us in a private, vertical arrangement. More often he works horizontally; that is, through a fellow believer whose various spiritual capacities are given for our upbuilding. No doubt many a troubled individual calls on God quite futilely while at that very time a fellow believer is failing to exercise his or her God-assigned responsibility of encouragement and help.

Such an arrangement means that our output must and will be of the same quality and quantity as the input. Pastors must see to it that members have a meaningful output. It is not enough to urge them toward deeper spiritual experiences without offering them more meaningful forms of expressing such new life. Surely the Scriptures not only teach how to obtain divine enablement and greater power in service but also give us definite directions as to how we are to share this valuable endowment.

We turn now to the public services. When members of the congregation are invited to participate, it hardly needs to be pointed out that carnal attitudes and feelings will attempt to rule. Some who ought to remain silent will feel the urge to express themselves. Others will shrink back, overcome with feelings of hesitancy and fear of being criticized, when all the while God might want them to share fully. Happy the congregation that can profit from Spirit-filled members, no matter how fearful their presentation.

As the members grow in their understanding and appreciation of one another, they will need warning about the danger of extreme passive receptivity as well as an opposite, critical resistance to what is shared by their brothers and sisters.

"I'm not a very strong Christian, I guess, because I simply cannot get up front and sing or speak" is a frequently heard complaint. Where did this "up front" orientation come from? Probably ancient theater had an influence on the early developing worship form. Despite all the warning in Scripture against immature believers taking up forms of public ministry, spiritual necks continue to be broken by falls from many platforms. Regular public exposure is dangerous to any Christian who has not been tested properly and set apart by the church, no matter how talented that person might be.

How It Will Look
Let us turn now to view the practical outworking of these principles in a body functioning with spiritual vitality. Growth will be seen in many spiritual areas, but there also might be a leveling off or loss in other aspects. (Cherished programs and activities of a church are not always those things specifically demanded in Scripture. Many traditions or popular programs, while not contrary to the Bible, are not demanded by it either. Perhaps some of these activities ought to be carried on, but surely a church must not leave undone any clear scriptural responsibility.)

Let us suppose that a particular church begins to involve its members in the public services and that personal ministry between individuals is flourishing. What outward, visible changes will occur? Probably, resulting growth patterns will show the largest increase in the midweek prayer service—assuming there is such a good meeting in the schedule. Next in growth often will be the Sunday evening service.

Hopefully, morning worship will also rise in attendance as it is upgraded in content. To the extent people develop the feeling that a particular service is "theirs," interest and participation will mount.

Wise leaders will take full advantage of evidences of new life to deepen the congregation's worship experience. Printed and sermonic instructions should urge members to begin Saturday night preparing for Sunday worship.

Arriving rested and early enough to unite in a planned congregational preparation period, members expect to meet with God. Every person is challenged to listen carefully to Scripture reading. It is the word from God to his people. No slouching in the seats. All forms of praise demand enthusiastic concentration. Peter speaks of the church's worship as a truly noble calling. "You also, like living stones, are being built into a spiritual house to be a holy priesthood, offering spiritual sacrifices acceptable to God through Jesus Christ" (1 Peter 2:5).

Another expression of spiritual awakening in a church will come in the area of finances. Quite normally, God's children can be taught to make a lifelong commitment to share generously with their Lord. Money problems will be ended for the church. Indeed, some difficulty of a very different kind might be experienced. Funds flowing in from willing hearts sometimes outstrip an assembly's maturity in deploying its benevolent and missionary investments.

Fewer offerings will provide more funds. Canvassing for pledges will be unnecessary. Public pleas and written appeals will no longer be essential. Again, underlying this welcome alteration is simply the attitude, "This is my church." It does not have to be said, but all feel, "We are giving this to our Lord Jesus Christ himself."

A commonly seen attendance pattern existing in organized, aggressive churches is that of the bottom-heavy Sunday School. I refer to the attendance bulge seen in the lower grades because of the greater efforts made in recruiting youngsters. Typically, an active bus ministry transports more children than adults.

Such schools with a decreasing ratio of adults will find themselves facing a shortage of building space and increasing financial needs. Furthermore, just as there is a lack of new contributors, it will also be harder and harder to fill positions for teachers and leaders. Very often an overall strained, tired atmosphere settles in.

Contrast with that, the church with a more solid, stable family emphasis—where there is instruction, worship, fellowship, and expression in ministry for every member of the family. Picture the focus as being on the home and on living the Christian life every day of the week instead of the typical emphasis on "this week in church" (meaning the building).

As this ideal is pressed into all the life of the church, discipline problems from troubling children and upsetting youth behavior will taper off. More wholesome teaching seven days a week in the homes not only will help the children but will bring forth more adult workers to help with the groups.

One problem will, however, develop. A larger proportion of the children will have their parents driving them to church, rather than being sent on the buses, and that will mean a strain on parking facilities.

If the Sunday School, along with the entire church program, is to become truly family centered, it will require certain steps of progress. For example, classing parents together who have children in the first eight grades will provide excellent opportunities to assist them in parenting. At least a part of their Sunday School hour each week should be invested in serious training in the following areas: every aspect of domestic life, family worship, and preparation for more effective teaching at home in subjects of doctrine, church history, and morality. No part of the hour should be wasted on incidentals.

Some churches have developed their own curriculum, even integrating daily family worship with the week's Sunday School text in a through-the-Bible plan. Regardless, provisions for training during a portion of the hour should be made by each local church for the benefit of their families. A top priority of every Christian assembly should be getting families to unite in daily worship of God and study of his Word. Sunday meetings do not replace that; they must provide for it.

New Leadership and Ministry Resources
Two basic plans exist for providing a church's top leadership: (1) grow your own, or (2) hire them from outside. How many of your church leaders came through the nursery or lower Sunday School grades?

Really, youngsters will not be the future of the church if they are incorrectly concentrated on apart from their parents. To love and provide for children will mean confronting the entire family with a serious challenge for each individual. Otherwise, young people will never experience real church life and will produce and reproduce only what they know.

Rich effects will follow these efforts. Maturing young people enveloped in this atmosphere will, in increasing numbers, tend to marry within the local Christian community. Stability will mark the church as young couples choose to settle in the area. The fellowship will be populated with more workers who are seasoned self-starters. Those offering themselves to full-time ministries will have the benefit of mature counsel and deeper prayer support from friends who know them thoroughly and love them dearly.

5

A Complete Scheme for Receiving and Recovering Members

My people have been lost sheep; their shepherds have led them astray and caused them to roam on the mountains. They wandered over mountain and hill and forgot their own resting place.

—Jer. 50:6

The proverbial expression "Easy come, easy go" is never more true than when applied to receiving new members into a church. Even more seriously, whatever difficulties might already exist in the fellowship are likely to be compounded if unprepared new members are brought into the family. As stated in the Introduction, a body that gains weight without new vitality is actually becoming weaker.

This whole subject represents a very demanding and complicated area of church life. It is little understood by most members and even some pastors. Every concerned believer should ask: Exactly what happens to new members as they are brought into the fellowship? How are they prepared? Then what?

Guidelines for Preparing and Receiving New Members
First, it should be clear that attention and effort given to candidates for membership is not primarily for purposes of

screening some out but in order to prepare each for entering. Full understanding of the church's life is the aim. The impression should be made definite that the church is willing to make considerable investment in the candidate's life.

In churches where public invitation is regularly given for church membership, it is better if the response is understood to be an *application* for membership. Those who respond are presenting themselves as applicants for the church fellowship. Such an understanding will give more opportunity to prepare them.

Second, proceed so as to overcome any predisposition on the part of applicants that they must be received no matter what their spiritual condition. This will mean confronting the phenomenon of "block movement," as I describe it. This unhealthy group movement often is created by gathering all candidates in a membership class without any prior, individual dealings with them.

An even more common and often embarrassing situation develops when a prominent but questionable "transfer" person comes along with, for example, certain very earnest Christian family members. Will not the problem person expect to move along with the others? The procedure I will presently outline should easily, gracefully care for this by placing the emphasis on the individual. Any acceptable procedure must be adaptable and able to meet needs as they arise.

Third, individuals coming from other churches should not be denied full help. The focus should be upon *them*, not upon a "letter of transfer." A realistic view of how things truly are out in the churches will forbid a receiving church from taking for granted the spiritual condition of any one applying for membership on the strength of a statement from another church.

Fourth, incoming children need and deserve special attention. The focus on youth and children of the church is best accomplished by constant encouragement and help to parents in preparing their own children through daily training and regular family worship. See my pastoral instructions, "How You Can Have Family Bible Reading and Prayer" in appendix 6.

For those homes where neither parent is a believer, sensitive efforts must be made to win the children and give them extra help. Where either the husband or the wife does believe, the principle found in 1 Corinthians 7:14 must be remembered: "For the unbelieving husband has been sanctified through his wife, and the unbelieving wife has been sanctified through her believing husband. Otherwise your children would be unclean, but as it is, they are holy." A believing parent is of utmost importance, according to this text, in bringing spiritual influence into the home. The church must not ignore but rather must cooperate, and work through, this God-ordained channel. The general approach will be to impress on the parents that they themselves have responsibility for their child's spiritual life. In cases where the parents are seriously inadequate for this, the church must arrange for foster spiritual parenting. Such an arrangement must be more personal than the regular programs of the church. Individual discipling is the most ideal approach.

Intake Procedure
Follow carefully the outline in figure 2 as each stage is detailed.

Sources of ingathering. These "sources" represent evangelistic aspects of various outreach ministries. The point is to get all the church concerned with winning people to Christ and seeing converts fully integrated into the fellowship. Newcomers and also those who attend but withhold their full commitment to the church are noticed and helped.

Fig. 2: Membership Intake Process

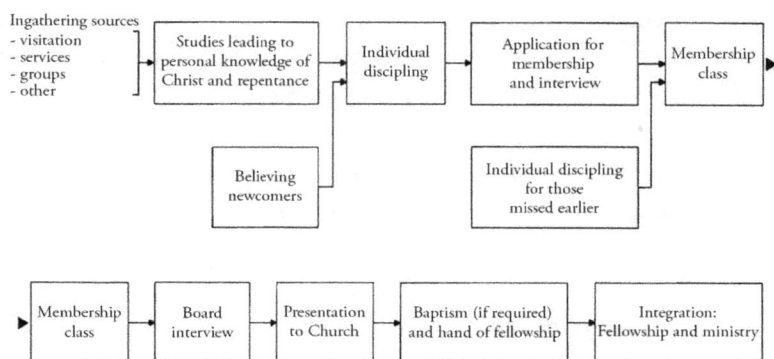

Ingathering sources
- visitation
- services
- groups
- other
→ Studies leading to personal knowledge of Christ and repentance → Individual discipling → Application for membership and interview → Membership class →

Believing newcomers

Individual discipling for those missed earlier

→ Membership class → Board interview → Presentation to Church → Baptism (if required) and hand of fellowship → Integration: Fellowship and ministry

First John 1:7 might serve as a guiding text expressing the two major objectives of this flow of persons into the church body. "But if we walk in the light, as he is in the light, we have fellowship with one another, and the blood of Jesus, his Son, purifies us from all sin." Those entering a communion of light will know both God's forgiveness through the blood of Jesus Christ and a new fellowship with believers. Thus there should be no hesitancy in prescribing all of the help delineated in our intake diagram. Properly represented, this vital ministry dignifies the person being thus welcomed.

Basic salvation studies. Leading to a personal knowledge of Christ and repentance, these simple Bible search materials will center on the person and work of our Lord and Savior.

Individual discipling. Here is the most crucial link in the entire chain. Both new converts and incoming mature believers should be offered this advantage. The very large subject of individual edification is treated in chapter 7 below.

Application and membership interview. Exactly what information is announced to prospective new members is all-important. The false sense of a group moving automatically into fellowship must be avoided at all costs. Thus it will be necessary to receive and handle each application individually.

The announcement should state that the church fellowship is open to believers who are willing to share wholeheartedly in the life of the church. Make it clear that they will be given assistance in preparing for the new relationship and becoming better acquainted with the church. Direct them to fill out available application forms. The forms then go to the proper shepherd for his personal-interview visit.

At the top of the application form could be a brief, modest statement of appreciation of the person's interest and also a promise of full assistance in preparing all applicants for the step. State that a shepherd or leader from the church will make contact shortly.

In addition to routine statistical data, it would be most helpful if candidates would put in writing their own response to several questions, such as:

1. How does a person become a Christian?
2. When did you become a believer? State briefly the circumstances.
3. On what basis does a person get into heaven?
4. Have you been baptized? When and where?
5. Concerning our church, do you have any questions you would like answered?

The shepherd receiving the application will then arrange at once for a personal interview to ascertain that person's true faith in Christ and readiness for fellowship with the church. If there should be any question, effort is made to care for the matter, as far as possible, during that visit. If needed, succeeding follow-up contacts should be made.

Not until each applicant in a given home is prepared to proceed are next steps mentioned. Any who are not already receiving individual discipling should have this opportunity made available. Such help will make the whole scheme doubly certain and beneficial.

Membership class. Next, applications are passed on to the elder in charge of the membership training class. It is well if classes are not noised about through announcements. Instead, it should simply be understood that they meet weekly, continuously cycling through the various subjects. This allows new candidates to join at any time and complete each of the several weeks of study. Here is a suggested curriculum outline:

1. Salvation—its basis and evidences
2. Establishing personal devotions and meeting temptations
3. The local church—its structure, privileges, and responsibilities
4. Getting acquainted with our church—its particular structure and ministries
5. Witnessing for Christ
6. Baptism and communion.

Overseeing board interview. When a shepherd is notified that a candidate in his charge is completing the membership classes, he makes contact with the worker responsible for that individual's personal discipling. If there are no special problems, the applicant is invited to an interview with the board. Of course, they will first hear the shepherd's recommendation, which is based upon the following: his own home interview with the candidate, the applicant's attendance at membership class, and an update on the individual discipling sessions. (It would not be necessary that all discipling sessions be completed before entering full membership—only enough to indicate that God is at work in his child.)

Presentation to the church. This should be done with both dignity and warmth. Involving the shepherd in the formal introduction or the hand of fellowship is highly significant.

Integration into fellowship and ministry. Church responsibility to the new member does not lessen at this point. Spiritual gifts must be discovered and developed. New ministries must be entered. This requires seasoned help from a sensitive, growing congregation.

Serving without Joining?

Using nonmembers in ministries and positions in the church tends to minimize the significance of a full relationship with the church. If a membership standard is important, it should be upheld. If it has no such significance, then it should be set aside.

If there is a hindrance large enough to warrant one's withholding a full commitment to the fellowship, then of course that needs to be settled before full communion can be entered. Until the matter is settled, such persons ought not to be given responsibility in the church. If there is no such issue keeping them from the fellowship, however, they ought to yield in love to the body and strive for unity. Those who would stand aloof for no significant reason, then, are apparently not dedicated to the life and ministry of the church. Thus they ought not to be recognized for a position or given official ministry.

With a little planning, a leader can approach nonmembers with a series of courteous questions ferreting out how they feel on the above lines of thought and placing the burden of responsibility upon them. It is not necessary for the church of Christ to be badgered by those who are unwilling to yield to positions that the church sincerely believes God has directed them into and has blessed throughout its past history. It behooves any believer when approaching a Christian communion to be humble and respectful to God's authority vested in that community.

Recovery of the Delinquents

All forms of church discipline should be viewed as loving initiative taken by the church in order to sustain life and relationship with the faltering believer. Humility and sensitivity are necessary in this ministry. The appearance of pride or a harsh, critical spirit is ruinous.

Since our God orders continuing attendance at services of the church (Heb. 10:25), a willingly inactive member is therefore involved in sin. The church (not the building, but the special gathering of God's people with him in their midst; see Matt. 18:20 and also 1 Cor. 5:4) is exactly that essential. One cannot both keep from sin and keep from the church. It is urgent therefore that absent members be sought out and helped.

Various types of delinquents will be encountered. For example:

1. Those with long-standing disinterest
2. Newer members who have stopped attending
3. Those fallen into overt sin
4. Those considered more or less regular members but who need encouragement to attend prayer service, evening service, or to be more faithful in attendance generally.

A shepherd engaging in a ministry of recovery will do well to make certain that his credentials from God are in order and that he is proceeding along scriptural lines. Ample biblical basis exists for this great work.

As an aid to one aspiring to the task of recovering God's wandering sheep, I would suggest a prayerful study of the pertinent Scripture references listed below. To perform this, write down the following three points, leaving room for your thoughts on the Scriptures, as they bear on each of the three headings:

1. Aim of the recovery ministry
2. Authority for this ministry
3. Attitude of those engaging in this ministry.

Here are the references for your study:

Matthew 18:15-20
Romans 16:17-18
1 Corinthians 5; 11:31-32
Galatians 6:1
1 Thessalonians 5:11-15
2 Thessalonians 3:6-15
1 Timothy 1:19-20; 6:3-5
2 Timothy 2:24-26
Titus 3:9-11
James 5:19-20.

Outline of the Recovery Visit

1. Approach
    a. Identify yourself with the church and board, even if already known to them.
    b. If they are still counted as members, express interest in them as fellow members, perhaps apologizing to them for

your slackness in not showing concern earlier.

    c. Watch for opportunities to have meaningful spiritual exchange, and be considering applicable Scripture for use later in the visit.

2. Message (points to cover)

    a. Outline their spiritual relationships—to Christ (Matt. 6:33; John 14:15, 21) and to the assembly of believers (Heb. 10:25). Lead into 1 John 1:7, showing that forgiveness through Christ is joined to our relationship with one another.

    b. Review the implications of the membership agreement entered into at the time of their joining the church.

    c. Seek a response.

3. Shepherd's decision. Make an on-the-spot, tentative decision during the visit. Here are the possibilities:

    a. This is a friendly call to establish ground for the next visit. (The great danger in this decision is that the next call might be delayed.)

    b. This is an official contact and might be followed by the final visit.

    c. This is a final call, since the member obviously wishes no further contact. After this determination is made, the member should be left with impressions of the seriousness of his or her decision.

Authority

Sadly enough, many churches in our day have allowed themselves to be at the mercy of the most wicked among them. Sinking in weakness, they have imagined nothing can be done to handle wayward members who are a living contradiction to what the church professes.

However, any congregation of Christ sincerely choosing to

change such defeat can do so. First, instruction must be given the church, emphasizing from Scripture the very positive nature of discipline. Even the extreme of exclusion from the fellowship is always aimed at ultimate recovery of the erring one.

Patiently, slowly, steadily, the shepherds go about their work, dealing with more recent failures first. Then, while keeping up to date with any new failures, they gradually reach out to those in other categories of need.

At this point the question will be in many minds: What about those who refuse to be helped? Are they to be put out of the church? In answering this, I would urge you to return to the list of Bible texts given at the outset of our discussion on recovery. Notice how Scripture lays stress on recovering the individual—even when excommunication finally has to be carried out. When a church defaults in this responsibility, it not only fails God but fails the sinning individuals by denying them the one thing that might finally bring their awakening and recovery.

In the final analysis, there is really only one cause for excommunication. One is put from the church ultimately because of refusing the help offered by those seeking their restoration. Jesus made it clear that, except for the sin of blasphemy against the Holy Spirit, all kinds of sin may be forgiven (Matt. 12:31). The way is therefore cleared for fallen believers who repent to be welcomed back into full fellowship. Refusing the loving ministry of the body is to refuse the Head, who taught his faithful workers, "He who listens to you listens to me; he who rejects you rejects me" (Luke 10:16).

The recalcitrant are in great jeopardy. Worse still is the danger confronting those who willfully disrupt a church fellowship. "If anyone destroys God's temple, God will destroy him; for God's temple is sacred, and you are that temple" (1 Cor. 3:17).

By now, the advantages of having a core of trained, dedicated shepherds should be very obvious. Realistic efforts can be made at recovering backsliders, and a full team of shepherds can offer personal help to many more individuals than one or two pastors could ever do.

6

Evangelism through the Local Church

A large population is a king's glory,
    but without subjects a prince is ruined.
                        —Prov. 14:28

A letter lies before me—one I have kept for many years as a reminder of a very wrong notion about evangelism. Written by the head of a good Christian agency, the letter asserts that "it takes a very special kind of person to communicate the gospel to today's _____." I will not fill in the blank, but you might supply businessman, student, military person, athlete, or any of a number of such terms. The letter then proceeds to argue that only a specialist like one of their staff members could successfully relate to the needy group.

But what is more relevant to people than other people? A church is made up of people from various categories of society. A brokenhearted laborer, overstressed executive, discouraged mother; the sophisticated and the simple; the artist and the handyman—a cross section of humanity—that is what the church ought to be. This gives the church great potential in its outreach to all the community.

The people themselves have various relationships and

involvements through their family lines, their residential setting, their school and vocational or professional contacts. This is why a good church has every advantage in evangelism. Witnessing is often much more effective when there is prior relationship.

Indeed, in evangelism the spiritual, vital flow tends to move along definite lines. Pastors should therefore look for individuals who can provide these living leads. Such individuals should be challenged, trained, and prayed with concerning their contacts. Then they should be assisted to move ahead in evangelizing their various circles of influence.

All this will require ongoing encouragement from a leader. At times the leader should accompany members in their effort to witness. On other occasions it might be possible for them to gather a group of friends and have an evangelistic teacher come and help.

When the laws of life are thus cooperated with, no artificial follow-up program will have to be superimposed. The womb that bears and the breasts that feed are normally in the same body. Apart from God's spiritual family arrangement, no mechanical aid need accompany any evangelistic efforts. Many dedicated specialists must struggle to see that their doorstep babies are at least fed. But the mother's own milk and love are without equal.

New converts growing up apart from the order and nurture of the very family that produced them will surely be disadvantaged. Even further, they will fail to appreciate and contribute to the body. Thus when the beginning of life is faulty, the self-defeating cycle goes on because those who are born and reared outside a local church family will find it more natural to reproduce in kind.

Yes, but . . .

Why don't churches evangelize as they should? The answer is not that they lack training in evangelism. Many have had much training but still do not evangelize. As already stated, some fiery evangelistic centers are populated with stunted, immature people.

Again, here is the key: evangelism does not provide for edification, but *a proper edification always provides for evangelism*. Close-up, very personal, individual edification is strong enough to pump new life into the veins of God's people. Nothing short of that will make them become self-starters in personal evangelism.

Sadly enough, however, this emphasis is missing from many, if not most, churches. On the one hand, some bodies are virtually sterile or seem to practice a kind of contraception! On the other hand, many are ceaseless in their activities of visitation and "soul-winning," but even this effort is inadequate if the focus of the growth challenge to new converts is simply to go and do likewise. Very large and very important dimensions of spiritual life are missing from this scheme.

Of course, evangelistic visitation out in the homes of the community can be a good thing. But it is a remarkable fact that, even without much blessing from God, such a program may tend to fill up church pews.

The vanity of an improper emphasis on home visitation is illustrated in figure 3. Here is the interpretation of this both humorous and pathetic drawing. The letters represent different categories of people. The NBTs are those who have Never Been There (i.e., to church). The next category of people, the WBBs, stand for those who Won't Be Back (i.e., those who perhaps will not likely return unless they are visited and encouraged).

For example, visit among the NBTs, and they will at least come once and join the WBBs. Show interest in the WBBs through visitation, and they will become HDAs (i.e., Holy Day Attenders). When Christmas or Easter bring special feelings over them, thoughts will turn toward the church.

Figure 3. Categories of Churchgoers

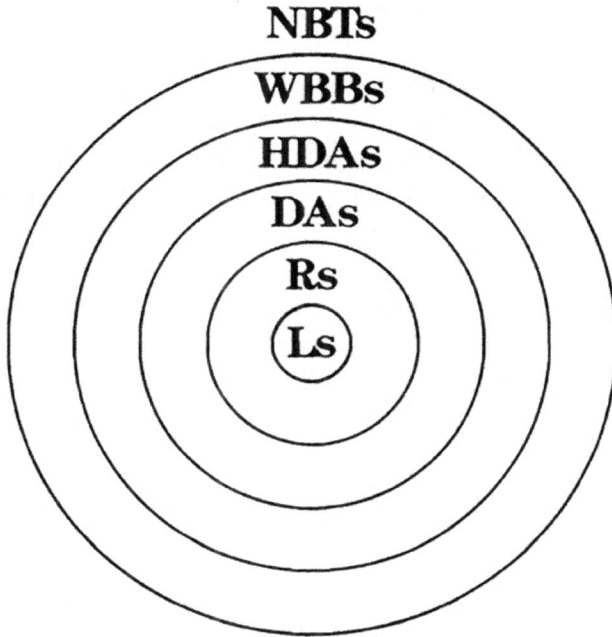

Furthermore, if one invests in visits among the HDAs, a number of seats will surely be filled between Holy Day Sundays, as some of this category move into the circle of the DAs (i.e., Decent Absentees). This group at least attend often enough so that their frequent absenteeism is noticed.

Finally, there are the Regulars (Rs) and Leaders (Ls)—but very seldom is effort made in really discipling them. In contrast, much investment is made among the people of the periphery.

Merely moving people into a less miserable category is not a worthy goal of evangelism. Remember the equation given in chapter 1?

Non-Soul-Winning Church + ? = Soul-Winning Church

The frequently missing ingredient is *full edification*. A deeper, practical form of personal discipling can both change the nucleus and also bring healthy growth outwardly.

Since every church is to be a spiritual family, there should be an all-pervading concern to bear and rear spiritual children. Growing by merely adopting members moving in from other churches is but a reshuffling of the divine population and proves nothing. The normal healthy church will have deep concern for its spiritual maternity section.

Methods of Local Church Evangelism

Let us now cheer ourselves a bit with a look at a variety of things a church might actually do in evangelizing its area. It should also be pointed out that, as the planned, organized programs are advanced, there must be no loss of the vision to upgrade individual members in their own witnessing to family and community. As these usable methods are listed for examination, you will notice that some will take place on the church premises, while other efforts will be out in the community—some in daily life and some requiring special arrangements. Here are the methods:

Individual believers in their daily lives. Not only those with a special gift of evangelism but all believers should be encouraged in regular witnessing. Men, women, youth, and children must be prepared for this. No church should dead-end their best energies solely in public programs to the neglect of preparing individuals for their daily witnessing. Leaders should study more effective ways for their members to witness on the job. Instructions might be given in creating opportunities to speak about Christ; for example, how to make tactful responses to a discouraged or complaining individual. "Be wise in the way you act toward outsiders; make the most of every opportunity. Let your conversation be always full of grace, seasoned with salt, so that you may know how to answer everyone" (Col. 4:5-6).

A positive, helpful attitude attracts those around and will give opportunity for fresh presentation of gospel truth to those with whom we work day by day. Often the secret of success will lie in arranging for a special contact outside the work environment.

Within families. Parents need encouragement to evangelize all their children. Because of the importance of this area of church life, see appendix 7, "Practical Help for Parents Whose Child Comes to Faith in Christ."

Definite, ongoing instruction must also be given to believing spouses to help them win their unbelieving partners. Members of the church fellowship should join in regular prayer for these needs.

Home hospitality. A dedicated family provides an ideal atmosphere for sharing news about Jesus Christ. Regular instruction and encouragement should be given in the church fellowship in this direction. Great variety in approaches is possible—coffee times, luncheons, more-formal dinners, patio cookouts, and indoor or outdoor game times. Relaxed, enthusiastic fun in an atmosphere of genuine personal concern for the guests makes sharing the gospel much easier. Questions and answers flow naturally back and forth.

Neighborhood evangelistic home Bible study. Each family of the congregation should take careful inventory of all their relationships—family, neighborhood, and other contacts—to see if they might arrange such a study in their home. Leaders from the church must be available to assist in advising or teaching. Again, this will require adequate training and a plan.

One creative idea is to launch the evangelistic group for only a specified three- or four-week tour through a Bible book or selected subjects. As the series is successfully completed, announcements might be made of a longer study beginning at a specified time. (Carefully avoid giving the impression of pressure or entrapment of those who expected only the brief series.)

Public services. A unique atmosphere should exist in a church gathering. Hearts of unbelieving visitors should be mellowed, if not melted. Any time sincere believers are gathered in the presence of their God—especially at weekly prayer service—unbelievers in the audience should have the feeling that God is exposing and confronting them. Notice how Paul describes such a situation: "But if an unbeliever or someone who does not understand comes in while everybody is prophesying, he will be convinced by all that he is a sinner and will be judged by all, and the secrets of his heart will be laid bare. So he will fall down and worship God, exclaiming, 'God is really among you!'" (1 Cor. 14:24-25).

However, the church building is not to be viewed as a mere evangelistic hall. Rather, it is the site where Christ's people meet to worship their God and to be edified. Here also is an ideal place for unsaved individuals to find salvation.

A very common and yet serious problem must be pointed out here. Rarely do churches giving public evangelistic appeals make adequate distinction between those who are addressed as "seekers" and those who are invited to become "confessors." Those convinced of their sin must be directed in their search for forgiveness in Christ. But also, those who are ready to stand forth and make their confession must be made certain of their foundation and then helped in their stand. The preacher can give this help to the unsaved, even though he is mainly addressing God's congregation. In addition, believers throughout the assembly should be watchful to help others find the way spiritually.

Scheduling special "guest Sundays" periodically will enrich the evangelistic heart. This plan should place primary responsibility on the whole church fellowship, with the one delivering the sermon assisting them in drawing the net.

Each "guest Sunday" should culminate in a coffee and conversation time after the evening service for all visitors and their hosts. During the day's services the gospel of Christ will have been fully presented and selected testimonies given to reinforce the truth. A warm and explicit invitation is presented to the newcomers to be guests at the coffee and conversation time for the specified purpose of having their spiritual questions answered. Members who brought guests serve as hosts and usher them into the fellowship hall, where attractive tables and simple refreshments are set.

The host members then enter into discussions with their own guests as the leaders move about the tables offering assistance. Such a setting both glorifies God and honors the whole church in its evangelistic strength. Often home Bible studies can be launched from this beginning.

Groups, classes, or organizations within the church. Any meeting within the church scheduled on a regular basis should be geared for evangelistic ingathering and regularly encouraged in such an effort. Leaders should seriously examine each group to see whether this is being done.

A plan sometimes used, but requiring much thought, is that of a two-section Sunday School. A school that is solidly family oriented and very serious in its Bible curriculum might tend to discourage newcomers—especially children of unbelieving parents. To offset this, following opening assembly, these children are gathered in special classes and taught a curriculum that is less weighty than the one followed by the main section of the Sunday School. Evangelism can follow.

Visitation program. Much training literature is available on evangelistic visitation. I will not seek to add to that here but would like to appeal to Christ's people not to give a cheapening impression by hounding their contacts. Instead, treat unbelievers as if they are fully responsible and explain that both God and you will recognize their decision.

If a man is disinterested or rude and resistive to a loving, faithful presentation of the gospel, ask him if he prefers that you not visit again. (This especially applies when previous efforts have been resisted.) If he wishes to be left alone, make it clear that he is really rejecting Christ. Ask him if he desires to be removed from all the church files. If so, agree to that and leave him with the serious realization of where he then stands. When this is done tactfully, but firmly, it honors God and is more in keeping with scriptural perspectives than doggedly pursuing people into the extremes of offense. Our Lord did not proceed that way.

Campus and military base witness. Student and military members of the church should be given much encouragement and instruction as to effective means of reaching their own friends. Innovative means need to be devised and followed out with enthusiasm.

Regular visitation at institutions such as hospitals, nursing homes, prisons. Many of these residents feel completely shut off from the outside world. Here are many hearts longing for help.

Contacting newcomers to the community. A welcome packet should be delivered personally to each new family as they move into the area. A letter from the church should be included, and practical assistance rendered where appropriate.

Community evangelistic crusade presented by the church. Scheduled in a public location, apart from the church, the entire congregation can be geared up for the services. One of the church's preachers could give the messages, with various members presenting music and testimonies, and all involved in bringing their friends and encouraging them to make personal decisions.

Family-life conference for the community. This also should be held in a prominent public facility and advertised heavily as being helpful and practical. After an evening of illustrated instructions plus testimonies by Christian family heads, the gospel of Christ can be explained as the simple answer—the one way to domestic peace and new life for all the family. Having been trained, the congregation of believers will have opportunity to help interested visitors at the conclusion of each conference meeting and later in their homes.

Sacred concert. This plan calls for formally printed cards of invitation with matching envelopes. The invitation would begin something like:

The members of
Community Church
cordially invite you to attend
an evening of music,
presenting . . .

Members mailing an invitation to their friends would accompany the card with a personal note of invitation to coffee and fellowship with them after the concert. There in the quiet of a warm home setting, conversation will turn quite normally to spiritual matters.

State fair booth. If an exhibit of this kind is attempted, it should be done with excellence. A unifying theme is an asset—something of common interest and easily adapted to spiritual truths. Related objects and statistics can be displayed, and perhaps a simple experiment or a self-test might be employed, gaining the interest of visitors and opening opportunity for one of the attendants to share the gospel. Literature must be available and follow-up arranged.

Neighborhood vacation Bible school. Moving this familiar enterprise into a plan of simultaneous neighborhood meetings often brings new opportunities.

Guiding Principles for Effective Evangelism

1. Keep the cutting edge out where unsaved are. Be untiring in rechallenging all believers to witness. Evaluate all programs of the church as to their evangelistic impact. Offer special help to those individuals who appear to have a more definite gift in personal evangelism.

2. Do not make exceptions the rule, nor make permanent and mandatory what is only temporary and permissible. All forms of specialized evangelistic effort should be evaluated in terms of this principle.

3. Believers of each generation and area must prayerfully ask, How can people today in my region be seriously confronted with the gospel?

4. The Holy Spirit inclines to work down certain lines. Study what these are. Develop these channels.

5. Guard against carnal delight in evangelistic results. Such additions are easier to identify statistically than are the results of

spiritual edification. Do not use converts as publicity pawns. New spiritual children should be seen, not heard and paraded. Pride in the very young can be harmful. Particularly, guard against pride in those who have status, wealth, or a notorious past.

6. Keep a balance between the extremes of overperfectionism and carelessness in dealing with the ingathering. Often Spirit-led outreach brings fruit rapidly enough to create two problems: (1) human delight and excitement, and (2) greater numbers than can be discipled and properly integrated into the church fellowship.

7. There are seasons in spiritual harvesting—times for sowing and times for reaping. Expect quiet periods. Do not then become discouraged and resort to cheap techniques.

8. The Holy Spirit will bless evangelistic work fully and freely where there is a deep level of prayer. (More is said about the crucial relationship between evangelism and prayer in appendix 8.)

Concluding Remarks

God is concerned about growth and extension. Without tiring, we are to "declare his glory among the nations, his marvelous deeds among all peoples" (Ps. 96:3).

This quality of service is not fully realized by either of the standard approaches: (1) bringing unsaved into services and capturing them for Christ within the church walls, or (2) organizing and going out after them. Rather, the entire church body must feel the burden and busy themselves responsibly in the evangelistic enterprise, following up all their leads. Vital believers of this kind generate an alive atmosphere, attractive to outsiders.

As for leaders, they will require more than abstract instructions in soul-winning. Surely their training warrants actual experience and involvement in meaningful evangelism.

"Look for living leads" is a worthwhile slogan. Indeed, it is the secret. Pray with each new convert concerning their contacts. Where necessary, assist them in the harvest.

Putting it pointedly, we could say that biblical Christianity does not exist apart from evangelism. Whenever and wherever true believers band together to form a godly expression of Christ's life, the pulse of evangelistic vitality must be seen and felt.

Nonwitnessing Christians are ill—too ill to be healed simply by instruction in witnessing. They need deep-down, all-around edification, such as will be discussed in our next chapter. Then, as new color appears in the saints' cheeks, fresh challenge can be given to evangelize throughout their network of personal contacts.Everything stands or falls according to the upbuilding within God's family.

7

How to Make It All Happen

Instead, speaking the truth in love, we will in all things grow up into him who is the Head, that is, Christ. From him the whole body, joined and held together by every supporting ligament, grows and builds itself up in love, as each part does its work.

—Eph. 4:15-16

Here in this crucial chapter, answers will be given to two great questions. These questions churn in the minds of hundreds of thousands of believers:

1. What is the real reason for weakness, unrealness, and failure in my church?
2. What can I do to change things?

Answer? The nature of church life as ordered in Scripture demands *continual personal edification*. All must participate, and when this is done, the church will live. Some of the Bible terms expressing edification are counsel, admonish, warn, instruct, exhort, rebuke, encourage, and comfort.

Allow me to make it very clear that I am referring now to private, individual edification, not to the various public ministries to groups or to the congregation. I suppose all churches engage in teaching, preaching, and encouraging people in congregations and classes and small groups. Very few, however, see to it that members spontaneously edify, encourage, and systematically disciple each other. Even public ministry is much more profitable to believers who have been personally edified.

Study carefully the biblical warrants, or mandates, for serious individual upbuilding in the following texts:

Acts 20:20, 31
Romans 14:19; 15:1-2, 14
Colossians 1:28-29; 3:16
1 Thessalonians 2:11; 4:18; 5:11-14
Titus 1:7-11; 2:1-15
Hebrews 3:12-13; 10:24-25

The Only Answer

Many church difficulties are solved only through widespread dealing with individuals. Here is a sample listing of problems that appear to yield only to the vitality rising from a more personal sharing of life:

1. The seeming inevitable and irresistible downward gravitation that overtakes the once fast-growing church.[1]

---

[1] Someone once commented to me, "It seems there is always an increasing difficulty with each succeeding group entering a new church. The first few seem so dedicated, but the next ones seem to have a lessening degree of zeal." My response was that the first group should be questioned and further helped. We reproduce in kind. God's plan provides for a continuing flow of life and power.

Another person, a worker with a Christian agency, once made the sad observation, "When a church organizes, the power seems to go out." Happily, I could point him to a nearby church where several dozen were prepared to disciple others in the church family.

2. Deeply hidden sin in the congregation. When the Holy Spirit is grieved over serious, secret sin in members and leaders of the church, the presiding presence of the Head will no longer be evidenced.

3. The vast, dismal ignorance among church people in the realm of biblical history and doctrine.

How to Begin

Remember that we are now dealing with personal edification. Two forms must exist in a healthy assembly. First, there must be ongoing spontaneous encouragement and counsel between members.

Edifying conversation does not, however, simply happen. Positive, helpful talk comes from those who keep their lives in good spiritual condition. Scripture must be memorized, meditated upon, and stored in the heart. Here, then, is the way to holistic edification: "Let the word of Christ dwell in you richly as you teach and admonish one another with all wisdom, and as you sing psalms, hymns and spiritual songs with gratitude in your hearts to God. And whatever you do, whether in word or deed, do it all in the name of the Lord Jesus, giving thanks to God the Father through him" (Col. 3:16-17).

The reason some believers are so attractive and helpful in the church is made clear by this Scripture text. No mystery remains. They simply go out into each day from a place of prayer and concentration on God and his Word. Many of them follow the enriching plan of selecting a passage or two of Scripture to share with others during the day. They are ready with a good, seasonable word.

In addition, believers are to seize opportunities to counsel those who are faltering or in some need. This responsibility must not lie only on the backs of pastors. Every member bears the burden for the spiritual health and prosperity of all the others. My book *People Helping People: How Every Christian Can Counsel* gives a more complete exposition of this subject.

The prior question now forcing itself upon us is, How can a church raise up vital members who will exert such a positive influence? Purposeful discipling of all key individuals is the way.

One by one, regular members must be approached and invited to share in a series of individual encounters which will deepen their understanding of truth and make them more effective in ministry. The plan I have used over many years is now in written form, entitled *Spiritual Life Studies: A Manual for Personal Edification*. The introduction begins as follows:

> Rather than dreaming of an elusive spiritual awakening that never seems to come, here is the pick and shovel of revival—a practical way of getting out in the trenches and seeing something happen.
>
> Years ago in the navy I watched the cook mount a ladder to the huge soup vats and stir them with a paddle of considerable size. Now, I picture many of today's pastors and Christian workers desperately trying to stir an oversized kettle with their own small spoon. New techniques of dipping, plunging, splashing away with the spoon are not needed. What is needed is a larger paddle! This deeper stirring will take place when the pastor broadens the base of ministry by multiplying himself. Many other Christians can be trained individually to become personal edifiers in the church.
>
> When men and women are dealt with individually, how different are the results from what is usually obtained in a class or through the congregational approach. This more personal, intensive method is often little short of wonderful in its effect. The workman will, however, have to keep his faith alive and put in real sustained labor. (p. 1)

Description of the Plan

Flexibility must characterize such a scheme. Here are some of the general objectives:

1. Make certain of the partner's salvation.
2. Stabilize and build up the life.
3. Where possible, get your partner to share these discipling sessions with others. In other words, you will aim at edifying edifiers.

A three-dimensional approach is ideal: comprehension, appropriation, expression. These imply that the one with whom you share must be led to understand each truth and to appropriate its full benefit in his or her own life. The partner, then, should be able to express each lesson learned in a simple, winsome way to others.

Taken together, all the studies should form a composite of the entire Christian life, integrating both doctrine and duty. Appendix 9 contains a listing of various doctrines and duties that form the fabric of my scheme of Spiritual Life Studies (SLS).

All these teachings are aimed at causing happenings in the life. New levels of growth will be achieved as God blesses the effort. The emerging pattern of progress will include the following six elements:

1. A more serious view of sin. Only those forgiven much will love much, said our Lord in Luke 7:47. Otherwise, we are a coldhearted generation somewhat like the older brother in Luke 15, who did not realize the joy of his father's embrace.

2. A new view of our identity with Christ. The substitution of Jesus Christ in dying for us as a sin offering enables God to look on us as having been duly executed for these crimes and raised up to a new life with our God.

3. The filling of the Holy Spirit. Just as our Savior offered himself instead of us, so now the Holy Spirit works in our lives to make things real in our experience.

4. Our place and ministry in the church. No independent attitude will do. Each man and woman must wholeheartedly give themselves to this great fellowship planned by God. God dwells there in special power.

5. The spiritual warfare. It is so wrong to leave people harassed and exposed to unidentified spiritual evils! The spiritual life involves a war, and believers need preparation.

6. Intercessory prayer. Ideally, lessons on this great subject should come early and be reinforced again and again throughout one's life.

Consider the versatility of such a discipling scheme. Problems in scheduling are minimal, since only two individuals are involved. Early morning, late at night, before or after meetings, at either home—all are possibilities. I strongly advise giving primary consideration to reaching first the regulars of the church—especially the officers and leaders. After some of these are able to lead sessions, begin branching out to others. Include all those coming into membership, new converts, and members who have grown disinterested or who are weak and fallen.

Sometimes it will turn out that the disciple is really not a believer. If, however, the discipling plan being followed is versatile enough, the leader will simply scale things down to whatever level is necessary for reaching the partner.

Expect Opposition

Whoever dedicates himself or herself to begin this program of personal edification in the church will face testing from a number of sources:

- One's own natural reticence
- Reticence of those needing discipling (this, however, is much less than might be expected)
- Very great inertia of the church program, which generally flows almost counter to this spiritual expression
- Strong opposition from Satan, diverting and hindering.

Before leaving our subject of personal edification, think for a moment about the possibilities existing if regular discipling is taking place in a church fellowship. When there is a drift away from services on summer Sundays, here is what is needed. If there are too few at prayer services, individual discipling can revive the appetite for prayer.

Wherever people show promising potential and yet are not involved in ministry, individual contact is a good way to change that. Or if there is a leadership shortage, then why not deal individually with the more mature believers and lead them to a point of useful responsibility? When the church's life overgrows the level of edification and multiplication of leaders, everything might seem quite enjoyable for a time. Increasing numbers and a glowing "success" reputation are exhilarating, but death is nonetheless on the way.

Full-Orbed and Full-Cycle

Getting everything going is not enough. Will it keep going? is the important question. If the program machinery is unplugged, will death come?

Death hovers near each apparently growing church until the leaders are able both to handle their ministries and also to reproduce themselves. They must have the capacity and vision to edify and integrate other leaders into the life and ministry of the fellowship.

The spiritual origin of leaders must be understood with great clarity. Putting it negatively: (1) They do not generally happen to move into an area all prepared to provide sensitive, strong ministry; (2) they do not simply grow, or mature with age, through a kind of natural process; (3) they are not produced by any ordinary program of Christian education—not even typical leadership training efforts.

Rather, godly leaders emerge when they are "worked upon" by a fellow believer. This discipling of those who will direct the congregation's life will have to touch and upgrade every area of their life, including personal attitudes, home and family responsibilities, and all relationships and ministries in the church.

Until all this is practiced as a very fundamental of spiritual existence, the church's life has not come full-cycle. No matter how well things are going, the congregation is a victim of an unrealistic dream. They perhaps have money enough to hire in more staff to invigorate lagging programs, but the body is unable to sustain its own life. Remove the catalyst—the successful pastor—and everything begins to wind down.

A church will operate with apparent health—maybe even for many years—if the orb of its gifted ministries is developed. However, its life is not full-cycle until its key leadership is reproducing itself. Without that, even the "good church" ultimately will have but two alternatives: live on the machine (the program pump) or die.

A plan of thorough discipling that provides for the upbuilding of the leadership will also relieve many defects and needs of the general membership. Most problems respond readily to consistent individual edification. Even when the congregation suffers from staggering marital stresses and many members are wayward or disgruntled, personal discipling can bring reclamation and freedom.

Now consider the promising fact that all those persons who have been discipled properly will *pray*, and they can be counted on to capture their fellows to join in a new pursuit of God and his purposes.

Testimonies to the Power of SLS

Following are excerpts from actual correspondence regarding Spiritual Life Studies—the first from a pastor. the second from a seminarian. Notice the multiplication and lasting quality of the fruit.

> Dr. B,
> There are encouraging developments on the discipleship front. One young father was a speaker at a father/daughter event last year, and while attending and hearing him speak, I thought, "This brother needs Spiritual Life Studies!" so I approached him later. Since then, we went through SLS. This year, at the same event, he was the speaker again. What a difference! Plus, he has begun taking another man through it.
>
> I just finished studies with a principal in a local elementary school, and we meet in about 15 minutes to ready him for taking another man through. He has eagerly taken the truths home and shared them with his wife and sons. It has been a joy.
>
> One of the ladies that was taken through by a lady that my wife took through is continuing to take other women through it. She is now branching out to try two women at the same time (not in the same sessions but during the same time period). She is committed to it.
>
> Also, one of our elders I got to with SLS has just finished taking a gentleman through. Great enthusiasm and seemingly real progress!

I know you are praying and wanted you to hear some of the good answers that God is giving us. Plenty of challenges and discouragements too, but God is giving victory in some lives, and I thank Him for it!

Dear Dr. Burchett,
I have been handing out your books here at seminary and encouraging people to disciple. I started the Spiritual Life Studies with a student from California. He attended a church nearby before he returned to California. That church started a new church near the seminary. My wife and I attended the church and talked with the pastor. The pastor knew the student that I had been sharing the SLS with, and that student had told him what a blessing it was.

The pastor then told me that a man in the new church did something very similar. I met that man today. For the past 20 years he has been discipling men (one or two at a time) using a study in John. He learned that study while he attended a church plant near Brown University—from a man who was discipled by R.P., who was discipled by you! The church plant was a "bud" from the church you pastored. What a small world!!! What a blessing—the number of lives that have been touched.

Heart of the Pastor

A pastor must keep life in the church reproducing itself, thus he must be a true self-starter. The draft always pulls downward, therefore someone must bear the ultimate responsibility of keeping the cycle of life continuing. Some of the drives of a church planter must be in this man of God. Each week he should take inventory and ask himself, What have I done this week to set forward the work of discipling in our church? Probably he will not be supported in this ministry of ultimate importance, but the responsibility is his.

To undergird all, the church membership files need to be organized into categories like this:

1. Those awaiting individual discipling
2. Those being discipled
3. Those who have completed Spiritual Life Studies, A Basic 13-Week Scheme which I authored
4. An index of those leading others in these sessions.

Two final admonitions must be faced by those who pastor. First, since a church is composed of the Lord Jesus as Head and all the members who make up his body, it follows that members most adjacent to us in the body will receive the most immediate impulses of life flowing from the Head through us to them. It is a ruling fact of body life that no member can give a greater flow of vitality to more distant members than one gives, for example, to his immediate family.

Second, true life reproduces itself. Pastors should do the same. I have ever held to this maxim: A pastor does not know as much as he needs to know until he is able to train others to do what he does. Schools may help, but pastors must bear their own responsibility for this.

Furthermore, the movement of life will not be limited to the growth and purity of the one church. It will expand outward into genuine missionary ventures.

8

Continuing Expansion of the Local Church—Part 1

Jesus replied, "Let us go somewhere else—to the nearby villages—so I can preach there also. That is why I have come."
—Mark 1:38

L ife has a way of bursting through the seams. The church lives as an assembly actively worshiping the Lord God and ministering to one another. Service to God is continually upgraded through ongoing training and full-orbed edification. A local church is simply a family whose members are in fellowship with one another. Furthermore, it is a kind of body that grows inwardly and outwardly. Christ founded his church as an expanding body. Multiplication is an essential function of its very life, not just an aspect of its program.

New believers (and also older ones!) should be converted into this way of thinking and living. Always there is the double role: edification and expansion. Churches formed with this view of corporate life will expand in more than a merely surface manner. True church expansion goes beyond a surface extension. "Consolidated enlargement" might be a good term for it. This will be made clearer as we proceed.

Arms

Broadly considered, the expanding outreach of a local church should develop in two forms: the church reaches out directly through its own local life; second, the church can reach out through gifted individuals—its emissaries—sent to more distant areas. Each church needs these two arms.

Hindering the sharing of Christ's life and light with distant people are many staggering problems and discouraging bottlenecks. Billions still are without contact with the gospel. What has stymied the church of Christ?

One good missionary organization, supported by many fine churches, frankly published a disappointing evaluation of its past missionary efforts. Many, many years had been invested in trying to plant the church in a dark area of the world. But after hundreds of missionaries had reported thousands of converts over the years, no real church life existed at the time of the sad confession. Rather, the whole enterprise was still dependent on foreign leadership.

Without a doubt, this failure could be explained in terms of the awesome resistance in that area to everything Christian. However true that might be, another trouble source exists that is overlooked by many.

A root difficulty lies back in the missionaries' own home church. Is *their* life and strength enough to sustain immediate, direct expansion of its own life? If not, how can life be shared in more distant regions?

And how can members of these churches qualify as missionary leaders world around? May we expect blessings and divine success in exporting that which we are not able to practice at home, where the supply lines are much shorter and the conditions so favorable?

Before looking abroad, let us turn back for another quick survey of the church scene here in the West. Sometimes I hear it said, "We are starting a new church here, right in our neighborhood." Think over the implications of that expression. As people build a supermarket in the new residential area, shall any zealous believers decide that having their own new church is also in order? A most important question is now before us.

By What Authority?

Deciding where and when there shall be an implantation of Christ's body is an imposing responsibility. Christ's body on earth should be established in the manner he prescribes. He is Head. He is in charge. Somehow, we have learned to do things "for him" in our own wisdom.

At the outset of the discussion, let me say that I do not admire the "shingle method" of church establishment. This is the approach whereby a building or temporary meeting place is obtained and the shingle or sign is hung out advertising an agenda of meetings. Next, the surrounding community is plied with invitations to come and fill up the pews and activate the program. Sometimes presumption marks and mars this approach, and the indictment of Colossians 2:19 seems apropos: "He has lost connection with the Head, from whom the whole body, supported and held together by its ligaments and sinews, grows as God causes it to grow."

It would appear there are two basic church-planting schemes that God owns and blesses by his Holy Spirit. First, local assemblies may expand outward in normal, living-cell development. Each new outgrowth eventually becomes a self-sufficient nucleus for still further development.

A second means of establishing local churches that has biblical authority is by means of missionary-evangelists who have been duly commissioned by a church. In biblical times evangelists were itinerant preachers and fellow laborers with the apostles. (All apostles were evangelists, but not all evangelists were apostles.) In the more permanent sense of the function today, an evangelist is one who creates new beachheads for the gospel, penetrating Satan's territory as an outreach workman. Our missionary-evangelists are examples.

In a less technical sense the term "evangelist" might be applied loosely to those in local churches who have a particular spiritual ability in soul-winning. Perhaps it is not altogether improper to use the term when referring to an itinerant preacher whose messages focus on converting unbelievers to Christ.

However, Scripture seems to emphasize these major responsibilities of the true evangelist:

1. Salvation of sinners
2. Teaching and gathering the converts into living assemblies, or churches
3. Continuing ministry of watching and guarding developing churches.

Thus, at the outset an evangelist might be training or overseeing elders in a new work. As the fellowship becomes more established, the evangelist would phase out his ministry and would be available only as required or requested.

Direct Ministries of Extension

Through its immediate activities and through its own resident evangelists, directing expansion into outlying areas, every local church should be engaged in outgrowth. Indirect efforts in expansion into distant lands will be considered later.

The rule is that every church should be as directly involved in extension as possible. A church of Jesus Christ must never stand to the side while others enter the church's areas of responsibility and function instead of God's congregation. *A church service is not a meeting for raising funds to support agencies to do works that the church is supposed to do.*

With eagerness, the church must take up all its ministries and grow outwardly, extending and multiplying itself into other fellowships. When its own local life is not virile and full-orbed as it ought to be, this first form—direct expansion—will hardly take place. Furthermore, the second form of extension (indirect church planting through missionary evangelists) will ultimately show flaws traceable to the homeland.

A look back into church history might help us at this point. Apparently there is no clear evidence of large separate buildings dedicated as Christian worship centers in the early days of Christianity's expansion throughout the Roman Empire. Evidence exists of quarters being devoted to this purpose in private homes. Perhaps some three hundred years passed before the custom of building centers for large congregational meetings became anything like a trend.

This lack of archaeological evidence of large church structures seems to fit with the biblical data as well. Romans 16, for example, accords with other historical data that suggest dozens of elders led the church existing in various sections of Rome. It was one church but had numbers of segments— each with its own leadership. Our goal now will be to see how the contemporary Christian church can exist as an expanding corporation of life.

Four Forms of Church Development
It is important to remember that a congregation's method of expansion will reveal and demonstrate its own definition and philosophy of church life. (See fig. 4.)

Figure 4. Forms of Church Development

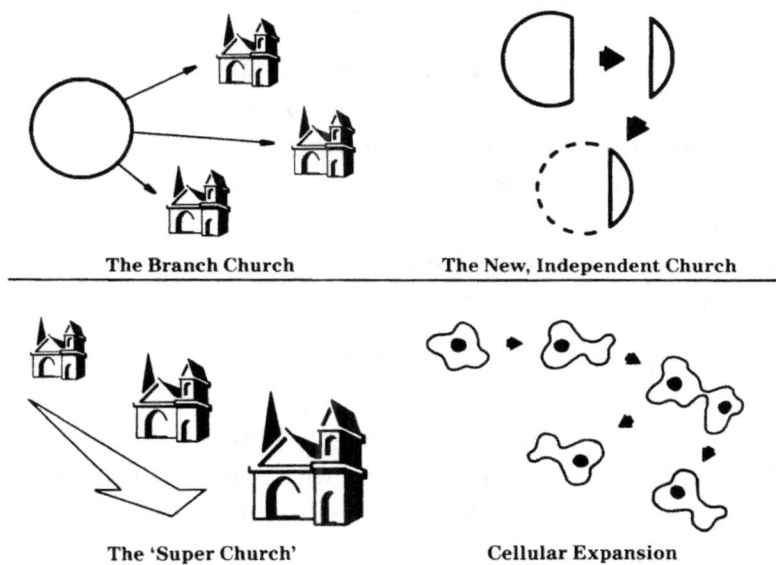

| The Branch Church | The New, Independent Church |

| The 'Super Church' | Cellular Expansion |

The branch church plan. Here a growing church raises up smaller chapels in outlying districts where Sunday Schools may be established or members assembled for worship. Usually, members in the branch remain listed as members of the "mother church." Sometimes a branch might become independent, but often the main church permanently governs the branches it constructs.

The new, independent church approach. Here a definite decision is made to form a new church, the members involved are set apart for that, a building is located, a pastor is secured, and a full schedule is begun. The church is born into independence. Critical problems might arise if the amputation from the main church is too radical. See appendix 10 for a detailed account of one approach actually taken to the birthing of a "daughter" church.

These modifications are called for if one at holds the principles of a developed church in its segmented, cellular structure.

The "super church" plan. In this common approach the church simply goes through one building program after another, seeking to accommodate its vast, growing congregation. Coming from many miles around, members often will miss more personal ministries to one another. Aspects of genuine life are almost always absent where there is a proud focus on the impressive size of the property and congregation.

Cellular expansion. This is the house church as seen in Acts and the Epistles. For more on the Scriptural basis of this form, see appendix 11. This conception of a local church involves a church existing as a main church but with numbers of residential segments, or potential house churches, meeting out in their own residential areas and also gathering for main services at the central location. It will be important, then, that all members understand the two-dimensional view of the church:

1. As a unified congregation of God meeting as scheduled in the central place.
2. As a main church composed of evolving house churches, scattered throughout all its neighborhoods. These fellowships of families will be known as "house meetings" at first—until their own pastor/elders are prepared and recognized and the members show strength in worship, discipling, and evangelism. Then they will be called "house churches."

Steps of Development

Here is a brief summary of the steps taken in the house church approach:

1. Develop the meetings into a sharing of body life. This is distinguished from a home Bible study and is different from a home prayer and care group. It is aiming at becoming a formed church. A schedule of regular weekly church meetings will take place in the house churches.
2. Develop body life inside and outside the weekly meetings.
    a. Shepherding in the residential area
    b. Hospitality and a full range of edifying discipling and interaction between individuals and families of the area.
3. Multiplication of leaders, believers, and churches. Proof of vitality and viability is reproducing. This reproduction will include new believers and leaders, and ultimately the possibility of beginning other house churches.

This type of nucleus-cluster growth may be understood by considering how plants like strawberries are propagated. An original plant sends out its runners, and other, identical plants take root—any one of which might become host to another movement of multiplication. Life is like this.

Blessings and Advantages

To all lonely individuals. These people now, in effect, will have complete families of their own—new spiritual families right in their own neighborhood.

Children. Consider their enrichment as they see their own dad or a neighbor dad leading the home gathering and keeping order, with other men and women sharing good words for one another. The sharing of problems, burdens, and emergencies will give rise to the sense, "This is *my* gathering!" All will learn how good homes are to function.

In truth, through this more intense experience of church life, all the children and adults are brought to a closer exposure to the Lord Jesus Christ as Head of the church, and Head of their church in particular.

Unchurched neighbors. These see more than Christians on Sunday driving by as they "go to church." Now, church life takes place close by, where they live.

An Objection Answered

Some will be uncertain as to the unity that exists between house churches and their congregational meetings. But the congregation is composed of house churches, and the house churches make up the congregation, just as families make up the house church. It is not harmful to the house church to emphasize family life. Just as good family life strengthens the house church, so good church life properly strengthens the congregation.

As the company of house church shepherd/pastors meet, their training will always make for unity. Then they will, of course, teach the same principles in each of their residential churches.

Conclusions

It must be clear by now that planting a new church in an unchurched area might well begin in a first home with neighbors. In contrast, if we begin with an already existing main church, careful and prayerful planning is required to develop its residential segments. In appendix 12, I detail all this in my pastoral letter to a main church.

Because of the large number of issues involved in expansion of the church, another complete chapter is devoted to it. Part 2 focuses on the church's opportunities and responsibilities lying beyond the immediate area where members live.

9

Continuing Expansion of the Local Church—Part 2

"The Lord, the God of heaven . . . he will send his angel before you so that you can get a wife for my son from there. . . ." Then the servant . . . left, taking with him all kinds of good things from his master.

—Gen. 24:7, 10

Before launching this demanding section, it must be mentioned that there exists a rather impressive literature on church growth. I do not intend to add more to that technical material. My purpose runs in another direction—to assert that missionary efforts in more distant areas invariably will display amplifications of any difficulties still unsolved in the host, or sending, churches.

We may not escape the divine requirement to begin at home. That is first. Turning elsewhere with the good news will neither compensate for problems nor work as well as we might think. Perhaps there is a law that says the further afield our expansion or missionary outreach is, the more aggravated will be any infections we carry.

However, each local church is not simply to continue to exist and grow a bit but must reach into outlying areas. The true church of Christ is powerful enough to do it, too.

Throughout history God has confronted difficulties in moving his church outward. Listen as Peter describes how God first shook him free of prejudices that held even the apostles cloistered and separated from vast Gentile populations:

> Right then three men who had been sent to me from Caesarea stopped at the house where I was staying. The Spirit told me to have no hesitation about going with them. These six brothers also went with me, and we entered the man's house. He told us how he had seen an angel appear in his house and say, "Send to Joppa for Simon who is called Peter. He will bring you a message through which you and all your household will be saved." (Acts 11:11-14)

Chapters 10 and 11 of Acts chronicle God's initiatives to move the gospel into new territories. The question before us now is, How shall the modern church reach those regions where it cannot directly minister?

Let it be said again that local churches should involve themselves as directly as possible on as many fronts as possible. Finances invested in other Christian agencies ought never be an excuse for easing out of direct personal ministry.

Peculiar and very special blessing rests upon any congregation that takes seriously its direct, immediate responsibility. Many functions now performed by outside organizations on behalf of local churches could be performed more fruitfully and with less expense if done directly by the local church.

Pastors of average churches experience sustained pressure from multitudes of Christian institutions and agencies, all striving for support. The pressure comes in the form of promotional mail and in personal contact from representatives of the organizations. All these challenges and counterchallenges leave pastors and churches bewildered as to what their own task is for the Lord.

Happy the converts who are won and trained directly in a living Christian assembly that has the vision of being a serving body for Christ. That church may find its credentials and even its very structure in Scripture. No other Christian organization has such an honor. The withering inferiority complex suffered by many churches has left them all but paralyzed when it comes to direct involvement in outreach.

Now, however, we are to consider the *indirect* ministries of expansion. Several guidelines are needed. First, wherever possible, church members should perform ministries themselves, unless distance is really too great. If special training is required, this should be provided rather than the unquestioning support of others to stand in their place.

Second, in cases where geographic distances positively prohibit a church's immediate participation, they should strive to send one of their own members as ambassador at large.

Third, if one of their own is not available and yet the church feels led of God to assume responsibility for a certain field, then let them invest in another worker specially chosen to represent them. Such a worker should then be embraced by the congregation as one of their own. A very deep bond of fellowship and service will develop. This arrangement would allow the missionary's family to spend furlough in a caring fellowship, much to the benefit of the church as well as his own growing family.

Other kinds of investments, while not wrong, should be thought of as exceptional and not allowed to replace the more ideal ones.

The Authority of the Missionary-Evangelist

The missionary-evangelist is one who ministers at large on behalf of the home church. Before appointment, he should be proven for many months, even years, in active service. So it was with the apostle Paul when he came to Antioch, even though he already was a trusted minister elsewhere. "Then Barnabas went to Tarsus to look for Saul, and when he found him, he brought him to Antioch. So for a whole year Barnabas and Saul met with the church and taught great numbers of people. The disciples were first called Christians at Antioch" (Acts 11:25-26).

This pattern appears in sharp contrast with modern volunteer and recruitment approaches and the easy church appointments. The proper way is for the church to prove the workman, confirm his evident calling, then recognize and recommend him to his ministry. He would then go forth certified and commissioned by his church. Paul was commissioned on more than one occasion. See Acts 13:1-3, 14:26, and 15:40.

The worker at large willingly reports back to his church as Paul did to Antioch. However, the church does not manage its missionaries. These have a unique, at-large responsibility and authority.

Not even the apostle Paul considered his authority to be dictatorial in nature. Notice his sensitivity and carefulness in conducting church affairs as recorded in 2 Corinthians 8:16-24.

He clearly admits his inability to manage his colleague Apollos. "Now about our brother Apollos: I strongly urged him to go to you with the brothers. He was quite unwilling to go now, but he will go when he has the opportunity" (1 Cor. 16:12).

Again, the Galatian Christians were reminded of their solemn duties to judge the doctrine preached to them— whether by the apostle Paul or by an angel from heaven (Gal. 1:8). Apart from Jesus Christ, the Head, no one has absolute rule over churches. This is further borne out by the Lord's word through John to the Ephesians. "I know your deeds, your hard work and your perseverance. I know that you cannot tolerate wicked men, that you have tested those who claim to be apostles but are not, and have found them false" (Rev. 2:2).

Contemporary missiology says less about the authority and calling of the missionary-evangelist as church planter and emphasizes respect for the non-Christian culture. Waiting to be invited in by the national church to positions as assistants to indigenous leaders is advised. Great stress is laid on servanthood.

But authority and love are not antithetical. The real question is whether the missionary-evangelist is or is not called by God to lead in establishing churches.

Obviously, any area of the world where the church is properly maturing should have its own interest in extension. Western missionary-evangelists might not be required, but it is not a matter of skin or culture. Essential Christianity moves forward by sovereign, divine appointment. Better a foreign worker with true credentials than a national without them.

Again, church planting is a special calling. Like Abraham's servant, the planter is commissioned to search out a bride for the Son, and the evangelist will also be supplied with "all kinds of good things from his master" (Gen. 24:10).

Exporting Disease-Free Life

Pollutants carried abroad in the missionary stream have spread countless spiritual diseases in Christian communities over the globe. Sadly, these corrupting influences are too often either overlooked or incorrectly identified.

Consider, for example, the factors contributing to the plague of paternalism. The roots are not merely political or racial in nature. Appearing early in most mission churches is the all-pervading notion of a laity under ministering ones who hold a qualitative kind of distinction.

Not only is this wrong in the homeland, it is exacerbated

in cultures where there is deprivation. Educational and other advantages will then determine one's rise from laity to clergy. Many a faithful leader without these advantages, but with obvious ordination from God, is still considered to be "just a layman." Above him are the properly ordained, more professional pastors, and often towering over all is the mission worker. (See appendix 1.)

Curiously enough, those who stress servanthood and warn of the dangers of offending believers in the host culture at the same time are often guilty of continuing to talk of the "laity." Here is fertile soil for the varied manifestations of paternalism. Backing away from that which is taught in Scripture (the authority and place of the missionary-evangelist), while perpetuating that which is counter to Scripture, is worse than unwise.

Nothing very different can be expected, however, when the missionary's homeland is peppered with lay-training places and programs. What is needed is not more rationalizing and explaining but root, fundamental change in the way the body of Christ is viewed.

Leadership authority in the church is such that, whatever one can do in more difficult and distant areas, one can (and surely must) see accomplished in his own home area. All that has preceded these chapters on expansion has been dedicated toward the purifying and revitalization of the home church. Unless the source is pure, the outflow will not be right.

Churches that are strong and true should be very careful to maintain good principles and policies in all their outreach ministries. They must multiply healthy, living assemblies and not merely engage in endless good efforts "out there on the mission field."

Put simply, the aim of missions is to see men and women

won to Christ and established in local churches. In some regions the church meetings will take place in underground home churches, while other nations might allow more prominent, public assembly.

A missionary is one who works to see this aim accomplished. The missionary-evangelist is not a pastor of any local church. Local national believers lead their own churches. The church planter sees to the establishment of the church.

As the church sends out its representatives into a mission field, it is everyone's responsibility to aim at the upbuilding of Christ's body. And the body of Christ is constituted in local assemblies, each bearing a corporate likeness to the whole. Merely multiplying scattered, isolated believers is not the biblical ideal. As said earlier, it is most normal when the womb that bears and the breasts that feed are in the same body. Little delight should be taken in delivering newborns on scattered doorsteps.

When the evangelist's work aims at establishing evangelizing churches, a healthy cycle follows. The local church joins in the expansion process.

Of course, there are many contributing ministries to this upbuilding. Any work is a good work that brings honor to Christ, whether directly or indirectly. However, we must aim at the ultimate, strive toward the one goal, and covet those ministries that work most directly toward God's final end—maturing churches.

It would be extreme to hold that all sent into outlying areas must be church-planting missionary-evangelists and none could be specialists of other types. But surely there ought to be a strong proportion of workers directly winning and churching individuals. The many fine support-role missionaries must not replace the regular missionary-evangelist. Rather, the former must aid the latter.

Churches holding these strong views, however, must not be found opposing any specialized works that God has called into being. The condition still prevails, though, that all who are "out there" profess that God is behind their efforts; therefore, each local church has the solemn obligation to implement responsibly its philosophy as far as possible.

Guiding Principles for Establishing a Church Missionary Outreach

First, *know the sending agency as well as the missionary.* In some cases these will be denominational missionary boards, and in other situations they will be independent societies. In either case they are to be workers together with the church as it reaches out into more distant territories. Here are important questions to ask:

1. What is the stated aim of each sending agency? Is this aim pursued on the field?
2. What means are employed to reach this aim? Are the means really related to the aim? (The Bible has something to say regarding the means and methods of doing missionary work.)
3. Is the individual missionary under support of the church earnestly and efficiently serving toward the proper aim?

Churches must not default in the matter of knowing their missionary personnel and being knowledgeable of their work. It is not good stewardship simply to reason, "It is missions, so it is right," or "He is such a good deserving person, and the work is very touching, so we must help." All these statements may be true, but only those items that best fit with clear, sound principles should be placed in the church's budget. Otherwise, how shall new and young members be taught what missionary work is all about?

Second, *seek for balanced proportion in the church budget.* The missionary budget should not merely "grow up." It ought to reflect the church's philosophy of missions. Here are questions to ask:

1. What proportion of our missionaries are actually putting their hand to the work of forming local assemblies? What proportion are supporting or carrying on specialized ministries? Is there a good balance?

2. What proportion of our missionary investment goes to cover administrative costs? Various agencies list and report their expenses differently, but inquiry will be helpful. A church might be contributing to overhead or administrative costs in three ways: through a portion of their missionaries' support being deducted at headquarters, in supporting a staff administrator, or through gifts to an agency's general fund.

3. Is the number of items in balance with the budget total? An ever-lengthening list of small investments discourages meaningful prayer support. Smaller items should be handled under miscellaneous or as a one-time cash gift. A church should enter seriously into the life and ministry of every missionary it sends forth.

Third, *keep up to date.* A church is not under obligation to continue backing a work year after year without a sense of God's direction to do so. As missionaries return home on furlough, their work should be carefully reviewed. This will encourage them to press forward. If their field organization determines to change their assignment, then the whole matter should be reexamined by the church. In addition, whenever usual furlough time is to be exceeded, the church should make their own evaluation of the causes and of their relationship with that missionary.

A Sampling of Problems

More than enough difficulties to humble, vex, and stretch missionary and church leaders alike have existed throughout Christian history. To give some perspective on lessons already shared, I offer brief comments on several problems.

Unpopularity of foreign leadership. Antagonism abroad often focuses on the Western missionary leader. However, the missionary is supposed to be one sent by God. He goes as he is directed and should feel confident in doing so if his call has the certification of a true assembly of believers. Contemporary trends do not change this factor.

The biblical picture is not one of a group of foreign missionaries from a "homeland" assisted by "native brethren." As Paul continued to work, his missionary band grew from the various national groups among whom they worked. Roman, Greek, and Jewish individuals joined the mixed missionary band.

The main issue, then, is one's calling. From the outset, national leadership shares in planting and developing its own churches. The pioneer missionary-evangelist's nationality is not so critical an issue when he properly fills his role.

But his commission from God to evangelize and establish churches may not be surrendered in favor of the more popular style of assisting national workers. The attitude of servanthood is indeed imperative if the Westerner is not to antagonize. However, God's commission must not be abandoned.

Nationalization of the churches. With varying degrees of pain and pride, church leadership and ministry roles on some fields are being turned over to national believers. Is it really too naive and simplistic to hold that a truly indigenous church would never require nationalization? I think not.

From the very outset, the first converts should be led into meaningful fellowship and worship both with God and with one another. The missionary may not take over the personal devotions between the national believers and their God, nor should he preempt their group devotions or corporate worship. New Christians need help for both forms of devotion, but the responsibility is theirs before God. In time, the Lord will raise up those who are able to lead in every area of body life.

Agency and church misunderstandings. Very often Christian schools recruit students from secular campuses. In turn, mission boards recruit missionary candidates from the Christian schools. Local churches are not necessarily involved in this process.

Finally, however, because of support needs, appeal is made to the churches. In many cases this brings hasty changes from one home church to another, and even a switch in denominational allegiance. Such procedure leaves the young candidate without deep supporting roots. In contrast, when the home church knows the candidate through deep personal association, more help is given. The local church is in an ideal position to offer training and experience in service and then decide whether to confirm and commission to a specific field of ministry.

Designated giving. Though widely encouraged, the practice of allowing each church member to limit their giving to particular choices should at least be questioned. Often this approach permits those with funds to get their favored items inserted in the budget. Even where this is not so, the whole atmosphere seems contrary to that of a family of God prayerfully agreeing on their missionary responsibilities and carrying them forward together.

If some specialization in interest seems good, perhaps it could be realized by forming prayer teams around one or several missionaries from the church. The body could indicate its confidence in the total missionary effort by unified giving. At least, the vast complexity of the designated system of giving should be avoided, along with its frequently seen spirit of independence.

Deputation. Independent boards usually stress deputation by the missionaries to raise initial support and then maintain it through personal reports to the church. Most of these congregations are not home churches to the missionaries they support. Smaller support investments means spreading the deputation over ever-widening areas. Various arguments are commonly offered in favor of the broader support base.

First, it is affirmed that the missionary is thereby upheld by a larger number of praying partners. The question remains, however, whether members of all these churches may be considered as genuine prayer partners.

Second, some cite the benefits to the churches who, because of smaller investments, can have a longer list of missionaries. This seeming advantage will ultimately become self-defeating, however, as the prayer depth matches the more shallow and broad financial investment. (Smaller churches seeking more missionary investments should have little trouble arranging with larger bodies and sharing workers with them.)

Now consider the advantages of a local church's contributing a substantial part or all of a missionary's support. While on furlough, the family can settle in the commissioning church area. The demands of travel away from family and church are at a minimum. The church may then offer sensitive healing ministry and fellowship to both the parents and the children, and the missionaries can in turn serve in the church for a time. Beyond all that, there is the strong and mutual sense between church and missionary of belonging to each other. Such servants of the Lord will return to their distant posts undergirded with a concentration of prayer and vital interest.

Several principles stressed in this chapter may be seen between the lines of a brief exchange in correspondence, reproduced in appendix 13.

10

Is the Road Long?

Each one should use whatever gift he has received to serve others, faithfully administering God's grace in its various forms.

—1 Peter 4:10

God's ways lead to the right goals. He keeps close touch with those who walk in his ways. They do things as he orders, and blessings follow.

Authenticity marks the church where the Holy Spirit resides. Mere publicity is a sick substitute for authenticity. Yet we are much given to public relations, relying on it to stir things into the appearance of life.

The early church followed our Lord's own style of ministry and did not depend on such promotion. Indeed, Scripture shows many making effort to avoid public excitement.

Spiritual genuineness requires no particular advertising. People admire solid, dependable realness. That is the reputation we must seek. We do not beg our community for notice. In confidence the church continues its faithful service, having Jesus' promise that the public will "see your good deeds and praise your Father in heaven" (Matt. 5:16).

Certain leaders who live and minister far removed from actual fields of spiritual battle enjoy audiences and a resulting fame.

Techniques in publicity expand their influence. Where, then, is the body of Christ? Everything about a body that the body did not itself produce and foster by normal growth is a weight and burden to that body. If one stops pumping an unsealed air tube, it collapses.

Is This All?

Consider all that has been promised to God's Christian assemblies. Have we realized all? The might and glory promised to Christ's body—has it been achieved?

Peter characterized our church era as "the last days," in which God is to "pour out" the Spirit on us (Acts 2:17). However we may argue the case against undue sign-seeking, surely we must not stand weak and denuded of all evidence of God's very presence among us.

What is there about your church that cannot be explained? Is God there?

Church historians tell us that the entire civilized world was nominally Christianized in less than three hundred years after the last apostle died. This fact shows that individual believers felt keenly their responsibility to evangelize and that each church was a center of life and outreach. Not long afterward, things began to change, and soon men talked of past glories. Political manipulation became the weak substitute for God's power.

Today's need is not for dazzling miracles, nor should we stoop to reliance on contrived self-publicity and political control. We simply need God to reside in power within his temple, the church. (See Eph. 2:22.) The divine visitation awaits the putting of things in order.

Meditate prayerfully on the following texts, noticing that, from our very supernatural birth, all Christian life is very special and spiritual:

> For you have been born again, not of perishable seed, but of imperishable, through the living and enduring word of God. (1 Peter 1:23)

> His divine power has given us everything we need for life and godliness through our knowledge of him who called us by his own glory and goodness. Through these he has given us his very great and precious promises, so that through them you may participate in the divine nature and escape the corruption in the world caused by evil desires. (2 Peter 1:3-4)

> Now to him who is able to do immeasurably more than all we ask or imagine, according to his power that is at work within us, to him be glory in the church and in Christ Jesus throughout all generations, for ever and ever! Amen. (Eph. 3:20-21)

If all these things are not real in our experience, of what significance are our clear doctrines of biblical inerrancy and authority or our ecclesiology? All sought-after, and even arranged-for, human accolades are meaningless if we evidence no marks of the Almighty.

This troubling admission brings us back to the large purpose of our journey together through these pages. The following graphic shows how to move from weakness to vitality:

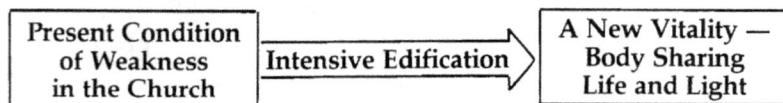

Present Condition of Weakness in the Church	Intensive Edification	A New Vitality — Body Sharing Life and Light

Bringing life-giving forms of edification into the heart of the church must take priority over all else. Four basic forms were mentioned in chapter 3. However, in chapter 7 ("How to Make It All Happen"), an intense, individual plan of edification, or personal discipling, was proposed as the key. Changes throughout a church will come with certainty where this is practiced.

A Little Test for You

Please submit to a simple examination. Discover for yourself whether the church principles being shared are clearly in Scripture and whether they are rooted in your heart. Read the following text slowly and carefully:

> Therefore encourage one another and build each other up, just as in fact you are doing. Now we ask you, brothers, to respect those who work hard among you, who are over you in the Lord and who admonish you. Hold them in the highest regard in love because of their work. Live in peace with each other. And we urge you, brothers, warn those who are idle, encourage the timid, help the weak, be patient with everyone. (1 Thess. 5:11-14)

Now make a list of all the tasks assigned in this text to the pastors, or chief leaders, of the church. Your personal benefit from this exercise will be much more complete if you put your brief list in writing. *Please do that now.* Do not read on until you have completed the brief assignment.

Next, with your list in hand, turn to appendix 14, where I have analyzed the same text. Are we agreed? Did you dignify the regular members with all their responsibilities? Or did you join the overwhelming majority, who turn all over to the leaders?

Now, turn again to the text. It is very clear, is it not? In giving this little test to Christian leaders and regular members, I have encountered a remarkable phenomenon. Minds are so enslaved by our traditions that, even when needed truths are clearly written in Scripture, eyes do not see them.

So it is that generation follows generation in a wrong way. The main body lies stripped of its very real spiritual duties of edifying and caring for one another. Furthermore, this defective traditional view turns every church into a two-tier, clergy-laity arrangement, with the so-called laity being excluded from much ministry. Pastors usurp nearly all.

In contrast, leaders who bring life to the body do not immobilize its members. According to 1 Thessalonians 5:12, they "admonish" and invigorate the members, thus keeping vitality at a high level so all the ministries will be performed by the members. Read our text again and see whether or not these things are so.

There's More

Consider this key passage about life in Christ's body.

> Above all, love each other deeply, because love covers over a multitude of sins. Offer hospitality to one another without grumbling. Each one should use whatever gift he has received to serve others, faithfully administering God's grace in its various forms. If anyone speaks, he should do it as one speaking the very words of God. If anyone serves, he should do it with the strength God provides, so that in all things God may be praised through Jesus Christ. To him be the glory and the power for ever and ever. Amen. (1 Peter 4:8-11)

The common, crass individualism—asserting one's self and own needs while refusing to bear burdens of others—is a breach of body life. Practicing love to others in the assembly is the essence of body life. Honor rendered to the church's Head is tied inextricably to practical deeds and help shared between the members. It is as the King says in Matthew 25:40, "Whatever you did for one of the least of these brothers of mine, you did for me."

Again, members of a healthy body have an awareness of one another. First Corinthians makes it clear the foot should not feel inferior to the hand, nor can one member say to the other, "I do not need you" (1 Cor. 12:21). Our individual well-being is intertwined with that of others. "If one part suffers, every part suffers with it; if one part is honored, every part rejoices with it" (1 Cor. 12:26).

Genuine fellowship is not a time of fun between Christian people. Fellowship is a responsible relationship of life. As the mouth serves the ear and the eye helps the hand and foot, so the ministry-need relationship is essential to the church.

All believers must be taught that they may not simply attend church. None ought to come unprepared to a single service. The typical scenario of the many spectators watching the very few function dishonors the Lord Jesus Christ.

It is true that the fewness of ministering ones may have something to do with the definition of leadership commonly held. However, Scripture does not allow leaders to have both authority and individualistic autonomy.

Mutual sharing of life-ministries always requires self-denial. If a proud attitude and sinful activity are forbidden, so are a proud attitude and "spiritual" activity.

> For by the grace given me I say to every one of you: Do not think of yourself more highly than you ought, but rather think of yourself with sober judgment, in accordance with the measure of faith God has given you. Just as each of us has one body with many members, and these members do not all have the same function, so in Christ we who are many form one body, and each member belongs to all the others. We have different gifts, according to the grace given us. If a man's gift is prophesying, let him use it in proportion to his faith. If it is serving, let him serve; if it is teaching, let him teach; if it is encouraging let him encourage; if it is contributing to the needs of others, let him give generously; if it is leadership, let him govern diligently; if it is showing mercy, let him do it cheerfully. (Rom. 12:3-8)

The atmosphere in a good church is like the spirit in a good family. To protect that wholesome unity, the apostle Paul was very vigilant, reproving the Corinthians for their party spirit, urging the Philippians to be Christ-like in their mind and temperament, warning Timothy and Titus against quarrelsomeness and controversy, and encouraging all to love. His classic word to the Romans reads as follows:

> We who are strong ought to bear with the failings of the weak and not to please ourselves. Each of us should please his neighbor for his good, to build him up. For even Christ did not please himself but, as it is written: "The insults of those who insult you have fallen on me." For everything that was written in the past was written to teach us, so that through endurance and the encouragement of the Scriptures we might have hope.
>
> May the God who gives endurance and encouragement give you a spirit of unity among yourselves as you follow Christ Jesus, so that with one heart and mouth you may glorify the God and Father of our Lord Jesus Christ.
>
> Accept one another, then, just as Christ accepted you, in order to bring praise to God. (Rom. 15:1-7)

The church that follows the scriptural pattern will have ample room for all members and leaders to function fully. A special beauty of symmetry is seen in a body living and moving in harmony within itself and with its Head.

Is the road long? we asked at this chapter's opening. Not so long as when we discard God's plan for a living congregation. Have you noticed how very early God brought these body-life principles to the apostle Paul. As a young rebel having just been dramatically converted, he cried out to Jesus, "What shall I do, Lord?" But the Lord did not give the information he sought. Instead, blinded and helpless, Saul was led into the city of

Damascus. "There you will be told all that you have been assigned to do," said the Lord. (See Acts 22:6-16.)

Later we see Barnabas seeking out Paul and introducing him to the Antioch church (Acts 11:25-26). Here in Antioch as a group of leaders pray together, God gives the apostle definite calling into missionary service. This is confirmed by the church's commissioning in Acts 13:1-3.

God raises no independent heroes. The life that comes from above involves us deeply in the lives of others. Enter this way. God will take you step by step. A body of believers has supernatural realness. And the church's Lord is truly present and available.

> But you have come to Mount Zion, to the heavenly Jerusalem, the city of the living God. You have come to thousands upon thousands of angels in joyful assembly, to the church of the firstborn, whose names are written in heaven. You have come to God, the judge of all men, to the spirits of righteous men made perfect, to Jesus the mediator of a new covenant, and to the sprinkled blood that speaks a better word than the blood of Abel.
>
> See to it that you do not refuse him who speaks. If they did not escape when they refused him who warned them on earth, how much less will we, if we turn away from him who warns us from heaven? At that time his voice shook the earth, but now he has promised, "Once more I will shake not only the earth but also the heavens" [Hag. 2:6]. The words "once more" indicate the removing of what can be shaken—that is, created things—so that what cannot be shaken may remain.
>
> Therefore, since we are receiving a kingdom that cannot be shaken, let us be thankful, and so worship God acceptably with reverence and awe, for our "God is a consuming fire." [Deut. 4:24]. (Heb. 12:22-29)

11

When the Bride Is Ready

. . . and his bride has made herself ready.
—Rev. 19:7

The bride of Jesus Christ must be prepared. Can you not help? Perhaps in our trek together, hope wavered as definition was given to problems. Remember, there is a great difference between constructive spiritual convictions and destructive evil agitation. Allow the one; resist the other. Let us now share important and remaining considerations.

Glorious Mystery

Two terms regarding the church are *glory* and *mystery*. Both apply to God's holy assembly. "And he made known to us the mystery of his will according to his good pleasure, which he purposed in Christ, to be put into effect when the times will have reached their fulfillment—to bring all things in heaven and on earth together under one head, even Christ" (Eph. 1:9-10).

This grand goal of finally bringing the entire universe under the ordered control of Jesus Christ is certified by our Lord's resurrection. Furthermore, the church is appointed to demonstrate this now! See Eph. 1:18-23.

Though we were dead, God has intervened and raised his

children to new life. We are now being edified into living quarters for God. See Ephesians 2 (esp. v. 22).

By its holy order and supernatural life, the church impresses spiritual dignitaries with God's wisdom.

> His intent was that now, through the church, the manifold wisdom of God should be made known to the rulers and authorities in the heavenly realms, according to his eternal purpose which he accomplished in Christ Jesus our Lord. In him and through faith in him we may approach God with freedom and confidence. I ask you, therefore, not to be discouraged because of my sufferings for you, which are your glory. (Eph. 3:10-13)

The apostle Paul makes it clear that his gospel ministry is aimed at making these mysteries plain (vv. 7-9). Earnestly, he petitions God that believers be infused with divine life.

> For this reason I kneel before the Father, from whom his whole family in heaven and on earth derives its name. I pray that out of his glorious riches he may strengthen you with power through his Spirit in your inner being, so that Christ may dwell in your hearts through faith. And I pray that you, being rooted and established in love, may have power, together with all the saints, to grasp how wide and long and high and deep is the love of Christ, and to know this love that surpasses knowledge—that you may be filled to the measure of all the fullness of God.
>
> Now to him who is able to do immeasurably more than all we ask or imagine, according to his power that is at work within us, to him be glory in the church and in Christ Jesus throughout all generations, for ever and ever! Amen. (Eph. 3:14-21)

Nothing less than the very likeness of Christ in the people of God will satisfy the apostle, who considers himself a servant of the church.

I have become its servant by the commission God gave me to present to you the word of God in its fullness—the mystery that has been kept hidden for ages and generations, but is now disclosed to the saints. To them God has chosen to make known among the Gentiles the glorious riches of this mystery, which is Christ in you, the hope of glory.

We proclaim him, admonishing and teaching everyone with all wisdom, so that we may present everyone perfect in Christ. To this end I labor, struggling with all his energy, which so powerfully works in me. (Col. 1:25-29)

The bold stand Christians may take against Satan's jeering—and in spite of their own failings—is because of the sacrifice of Christ on the cross.

When you were dead in your sins and in the uncircumcision of your sinful nature, God made you alive with Christ. He forgave us all our sins, having canceled the written code, with its regulations, that was against us and that stood opposed to us; he took it away, nailing it to the cross. And having disarmed the powers and authorities, he made a public spectacle of them, triumphing over them by the cross. (Col. 2:13-15)

What Do You See?

Beings of the spiritual realm see God's glory through the church. What do you and I see?

Study 2 Corinthians 5:14-21. Focus particularly on these verses: "So from now on we regard no one from a worldly point of view. Though we once regarded Christ in this way, we do so no longer. Therefore, if anyone is in Christ, he is a new creation; the old has gone, the new has come!" (vv. 16-17).

This transcendent view of humankind shows there are two created orders—one old and one new. Christ is to be viewed as

Head of the new. Believers, by virtue of their position in Christ, are the new creation.

The old order is headed by Adam and doomed in him. Christ enters the scene with the precious gift of new life. Study now Romans 5:12-21.

The only way to salvation, then, is to be in the body of Christ. He is Head of the new order. The people of God in the Old Testament period were saved by faith and counted in Christ. The New Testament commonly calls Christ's people "the church."

Whether new or old covenant, there is but one body of Christ and one way to be saved, because there is one Savior, Jesus Christ. All who have ever lived on earth or whoever will live here are either in Adam or in Jesus Christ. That is what Romans 5:18-19 is teaching and what the chapters preceding and following explain. This is the biblical worldview, and herein lies the real meaning of this often misused text; read it again: "So from now on we regard no one from a worldly point of view. Though we once regarded Christ in this way, we do so no longer. Therefore, if anyone is in Christ, he is a new creation; the old has gone, the new has come!" (2 Cor. 5:16-17).

This precious bond between us and our Lord is called marriage. He "marries" us out of the old order. Consider this Old Testament picture of the church glorious:

> Listen, O daughter, consider and give ear;
>> Forget your people and your father's house.
> The king is enthralled by your beauty;
>> honor him, for he is your lord.
> The Daughter of Tyre will come with a gift,
>> men of wealth will seek your favor.
> All glorious is the princess within her chamber;
>> her gown is interwoven with gold.
> In embroidered garments she is led to the king;

> her virgin companions follow her
> and are brought to you.
> They are led in with joy and gladness;
> hey enter the palace of the king.
>
> Your sons will take the place of your fathers;
> you will make them princes throughout the land.
> I will perpetuate your memory through all generations;
> therefore the nations will praise you for ever and ever.
> (Ps. 45:10-17)

Preparing for the Greatest Wedding

The myriad details in preparation for a large wedding tend to make the mind whirl and the heart sink. We are concerned here with a glorious marriage toward which all creation looks. A deep commitment is necessary.

If you have a will to share in the bridal preparation, then the principles propounded in the earlier chapters will direct you to that end. Review the teaching prayerfully, and make a life commitment to promote the welfare of Christ's bride. Plan your strategy of enlisting others. See that systematic edification is begun. That is the key.

Do not needlessly dent and damage the structure of your church. A bombastic iconoclasm is not the Spirit's manner with Christ's bride. If there is life, there can be growth. As healing and new life come, the twisted can be straightened. Old defective ideas and practices eventually will yield to light and love. Study appendix 15, where I give my own extended personal testimony describing crucial lessons that God clarified for me.

Then pray in love for your church. My suggestions for doing so are found in appendix 16.

Give special attention to the principles listed at the conclusion of chapter 3. Problems usually beset the way of progress, but take heart and hear what the messenger from heaven said to Daniel: "Do not be afraid, Daniel. Since the first day that you set your mind to gain understanding and to humble yourself before your God, your words were heard, and I have come in response to them" (Dan. 10:12).

As the church to which you belong is enlivened, you as a member will begin receiving new life and encouragement. Until then, God the Holy Spirit will supply your need specially. "The one who calls you is faithful and he will do it. . . . The grace of our Lord Jesus Christ be with you" (1 Thess. 5:24, 28).

Appendix 1

The Unbiblical Concepts of Clergy and Laity

The question must be asked, Is there anywhere in Scripture a basis for the class distinction between "clergy" and "laity"? The answer is clear—no qualitative, vertical distinction of classes within the church is taught in Scripture.

The popular two-tier notion of the church does not exist in the Bible. Rather, the distinctions given in the New Testament are horizontal ones. Differing offices and distinctive gifts are to be seen in the church, but no member or members of the body are vertically special and elevated above others.

Please understand that figure 1 in chapter 3 is not to be understood as contradicting this truth. The physical position of leaders in the diagram in no way is to be construed as elevating them to a spiritual position above their fellows. If it makes things clearer, simply move the shaded area to the bottom of the circle and replace the term *overhanging* in the text with *undergirding*. Thus, the leaders undergird other members.

Philip Schaff, eminent church historian of a past generation, has reported that originally all Christians could function in congregational meetings according to their gifts—whether to pray, teach, exhort, or preach. Indeed, under the high-priesthood of Christ the believers practiced a general, or universal, priesthood and kingship before God (1 Peter 2:5, 9;

5:3; Rev. 1:6; 5:10; 20:6; see also Schaff, *History of the Christian Church*, vol. 2, chap. 4).

The term *clergy* in the original language of the New Testament (*klēros*) applies to the whole body of believers! In 1 Peter 5:3 the leaders are warned not to assume a lordly attitude over the "clergy," the body of believers. Colossians 1:12 shows that all saints have the status ("inheritance") of clergy. Schaff goes on to trace the subsequent development of the notion of the "lower" laity and a change in the use of the "clergy." Not only were leaders exalted in the churches as the special "clergymen," but soon they were viewed as separated from secular business. By the fourth century, some appear to have begun using special clerical dress.

Even if there were clergy and laity in Scripture, it would be interesting to question how a layman might rise to the clerical category in biblical times. Once that elevation was obtained, could an elder or pastor—say, in Antioch of Pisidia (study Acts 14)—move to Jerusalem and expect to be received as an "ordained pastor" along with those mighty leaders there? Remember, these new arrivals would be recent converts, who of necessity had been striving to lead others even newer in the faith back in their home area.

The question, then, is whether ordination is a fully transportable status. Does not Scripture seem to suggest, instead, a reference to the local situation? At any rate, the notion of a kind of universal clergy status needs fresh, honest biblical scrutiny.

None of the foregoing thoughts may be taken to mean that the eldership, or pastoral office, is not special. Looking again at figure 1 in chapter 3, it will be seen that most believers are not leaders. Indeed, not all leaders are pastors. Individual believers serve in their assigned places.

The specialness of the pastoral office and function is not to be found in the full-time demands it might make. Some very fine pastors are only part-time—perhaps investing less time than other workers who are classed by some as only "laymen."

If Scripture does not speak of a special, universal spiritual category of "clergymen," then wherein lies the pastoral authority? The answer is very simple. His distinctive office and the authority to carry on that function comes from God and is recognized by the communion he serves. A true leader of this sort serves others by taking oversight of the assembly. Leadership is the most demanding ministry of all. It is a service to others.

The terms *elder* and *pastor* may be properly interchanged much of the time, but they are not exactly synonymous. The terms carry a difference in meaning. *Pastor, overseer,* and *bishop* are biblical words emphasizing function, whereas *elder* emphasizes status and dignity of the office, according to Scripture. (See chap. 3.)

Permit me to summarize where we have come thus far. The pastoral office is not set apart from the body or set over the body as if it is occupied by a special kind of believer, called a "clergyman," thus leaving the ones who make up the body of believers to be called "the laity." There is only one who is distinct from the body, above the body, and yet ministers to it—the Head, our Lord Jesus Christ.

Again, there are those sitting in many church pews who, under the power of God's Spirit, could serve faithfully, even mightily, if only they were trusted and trained.

All this is not to say, however, that the leader is not special. (See Heb. 13:7, 17.) All members of the congregation have vital and distinct functions to perform. Only pastors are pastors. They perform a very important ministry.

The clergy-laity contrast does not pose the only harsh

dichotomy held by Christians. Those who draw a sharp line between their "pure biblical flocks" and the more organized churches with traditional professional clergy are not always truly spiritual and scriptural. Sometimes even proper leadership authority is disallowed. Even more surprising are those who fault other church groups for a bishop-pastor distinction but never question the use of "laity."

Full Ordination Depends upon What?

In communions holding a definite distinction between the clergy and the laity, the definitions are vague in the minds of average believers. For example, how does one get from the laity into the clergy? Some feel that elevation is achieved once a member begins full-time investment in pastoral duties. Not so in actual experience, for many full-time pastors are simply called lay-preachers or lay-pastors.

Then is it a matter of schooling? Yes, often so. For example, "ordained ministers" with the "Rev." ahead of their names are in all kinds of professions other than pastoring. They spend no time performing the sacred task for which they were ordained and yet they are "clergy," whereas another earnest believer works at pastoring and/or preaching full time and he is still a "layman." Apparently, approved seminary training made possible this recognition.

This leads me to the far-reaching issue of the local church sharing seriously and fully in preparing its own members for positions of ministry. More creative use of institutions is called for, rather than simply allowing precedent from the schools to direct the church. Academic professors may be needed to help prepare pastors, but they must not take pastors' God-given commission to train and prepare their own congregational leaders. Local churches must break out of the restrictive molds placed on them and develop their ongoing leadership. Only this way can a local church go full-cycle in its life—by continuing to provide its own pastors, teachers, and leaders. Such is the full-orbed life Christ intends for his body.

Related Problems

Several major problems may be cited as contributing to power loss in the pulpits and in pastoral offices of churches today:

1. Possessiveness of the pastor who conceives of his office as a special, clerical one. He is thus left without a fully meaningful relationship with fellow believers, who see themselves as in the lower, laity class.
2. The congregation's reticence to recognize leaders arising from the pew. Hopefully this book will delineate a scriptural plan for handling this issue.
3. The leader's feelings of inadequacy.
4. False emphasis on servanthood. This misunderstanding is leading multitudes of ministering men to abdicate their authority and forsake responsibility. Thus we have the modern spectacle of pastors who follow after the sheep. When a sheep hears a nearby wolf snarl, he will not wish to see his shepherd down on all fours humbly identifying with the flock. Instead of so much striving to prove that he can relate and be a "true servant," let the shepherd stand up and be a leader. The most demanding service is leadership. It is also the most rarely seen.

Appendix 2
Spiritual Gifts

I n chapter 3 I sought to show that God gives certain ones the responsibility and enablement to develop others in ministries. And though all in the body share a common faith in Christ, not all are equipped in the same way for spiritual service to God.

Clearing the Vision

"Now to each one the manifestation of the Spirit is given for the common good" (1 Cor. 12:7). One's spiritual gifts are here said to be an expression of the Holy Spirit and are entrusted to an individual believer for the good of fellow members. It is important, then, to distinguish between a particular gift of the Spirit for service and *the* gift of the Spirit that belongs to every true believer. Study John 7:39 and 1 Corinthians 12:13.

Furthermore, a *gift* of the Spirit must be distinguished from the *fruit* of the Spirit—that enrichment of character produced by the Holy Spirit. "But the fruit of the Spirit is love, joy, peace, patience, kindness, goodness, faithfulness, gentleness and self-control. Against such things there is no law" (Gal. 5:22-23).

Still further, a *gift* of the Spirit must not be confused with *natural talent.* The two might dovetail, but generally speaking, natural abilities are one thing, and spiritual capabilities given specially by God are quite another thing. No one can serve effectively in the spiritual realm with only natural talents, and counterfeits are dangerous. The apostle Paul instructed the young Corinthian church in this distinction at the outset of his first epistle (1 Cor. 1:5-7, 26-31).

God demands healthy unity in the Christian congregation. However, the very diversity provided by the Spirit makes unity difficult. No doubt that is why the love chapter, 1 Corinthians 13, is set squarely between two chapters treating the gifts at great length.

Look at 1 Corinthians 12:4-7 and you will see three sources of variety in local church ministries. First, believers differ in their gifts (v. 4). For example, some will be like builders who work with saws, while others are equipped with drills. To continue the figure, look at verse 5, where there is difference not only in gifts but in ministries. Thus, some craftsmen might do rough, unfinished framing, while others construct fine-detail cabinet work. Finally, verse 6 indicates diversity of still another kind—perhaps in scope and intensity.

Church members should therefore not all strive to do the same things in the same ways or to the same extent. The Lord Jesus Christ must superintend his church. Still further, some allowance must be made for human personality differences and for much variation in spiritual attainment.

But are the gifts for today? Several answers are commonly given to this inquiry:

1. No gifts exist today.
2. Some gifts exist.
3. All gifts exist just as in the early New Testament church.

My position is a modification of no. 3. Since there is no one official gift list given in Scripture, a certain flexibility is evidently expected. As needed and required, gifts are available—some for launching, others for continuing in more mature orbit. If not needed, they are not intended.

A Brief Examination of the Gifts

Before presenting a general list of gifts, let me set forth what we could call the foundational ministries. These are the basic works necessary to plant the church, edify it, shepherd and protect the flock, and extend the work. Ephesians 4:11 enumerates these four foundational ministries.

First, there is *apostle.* The term carries two connotations. The Twelve, who laid the church's foundation and were vehicles for revelations of truth, were apostles in a special sense. On other occasions the term simply meant "one sent on a mission"; for example, that of assisting in planting new churches. This latter function is that of the missionary-evangelist today.

Prophet is next mentioned. The contemporary preacher who uses the Word in the Spirit's power fills this role today.

The *evangelist* referred to is not the same as the modern professional evangelist. In early church history evangelists were those who not only propagated the gospel but had much to do with establishing the churches. Today what is still required of the apostolic function of founding congregations for Christ in new areas is committed to the hands of the missionary-evangelists.

The *pastor* (elder) will preside and shepherd the local flock. Very often also the pastor will be equipped by the Spirit as *teacher.* However, not all teachers will be fully engaged in shepherding. Using truth with a primary concern for the believers' behavior is the pastor's concern. Teachers aim first at instructing in truths of the Word and do not have the heavy responsibility for the flock carried by the shepherd. Teachers fulfilling basic ministries might be settled in a single local church, or they might be given by God to travel among numbers of churches.

Romans 12 and 1 Corinthians 12 offer the two major gift lists. A somewhat organized and unified listing might run as follows:

1. *Prophecy*. In the apostolic day this meant speaking new revelation. Today it involves proclaiming the core of truth "once for all delivered." Even in the Old Testament sense, prophecy was not primarily a predicting of events, though that often was involved. Basically, the prophet is one who gives God's Word to the people. Now that the Word is written in full, the preacher uses it to shine as a light in dark areas of lives, thus the shades are raised and new light floods regions needing exposure and enlightenment. "But everyone who prophesies speaks to men for their strengthening, encouragement and comfort" (1 Cor. 14:3).

Figure 5 presents the relationship between the prophet of biblical days and the preacher in today's church—now that we have the full Scripture. Notice, too, that this kind of prophecy or preaching brings to unbelievers deep conviction and exposure of sin and to believers it brings encouragement (1 Cor. 14:24-25, 31).

2. *Teaching*—the ability from God to pass on truth to others in a form that instructs their understanding and fits life.

3. *Exhortation*—enablement to counsel, encourage, or perhaps steady a faltering believer before personal disaster and corporate problems develop.

4. *Wisdom*—ability to apply biblical insights to specific situations arising in the life of the church or an individual's life.

5. *Knowledge*—a spiritual capacity to understand and systematize truth for the church's benefit.

6. *Faith*—a certain belief in Jesus Christ is required of all believers, but the particular gift of faith is a spiritual endowment that enables some to function as "eyes of the body." They possess

Figure 5: Prophecy—Then and Now

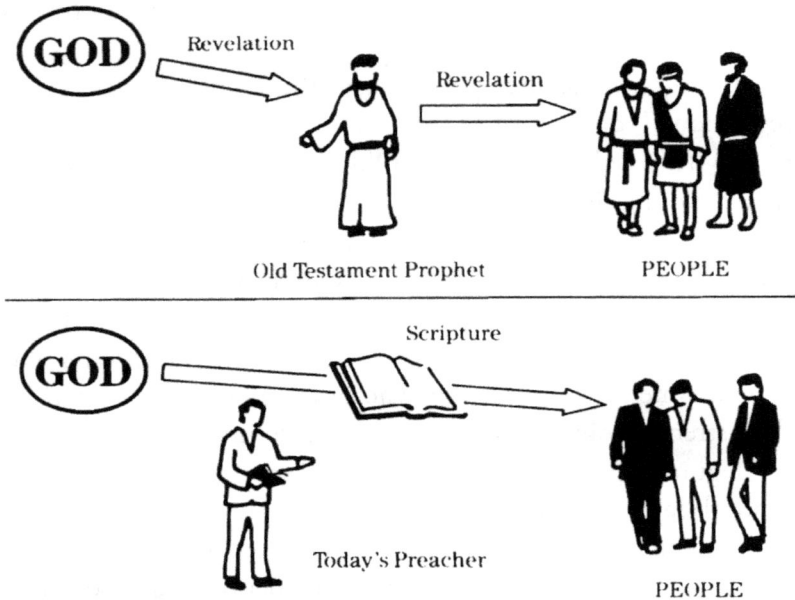

Old Testament Prophet   PEOPLE

Today's Preacher

PEOPLE

an unusual vision of the will of God and a strong confidence in his power to perform tasks at hand.

In some cases the person of faith will see the goal but mightnot be able to plan how the goal shall be attained. In contrast, one gifted in administration might be so concerned with mechanics that he or she has not the clear confidence to step out in faith. The congregation therefore needs them both!

7. *Discernment*—the ability to discover the true spiritual implications of issues and attitudes, to distinguish between what is of the Holy Spirit and what is merely a production of human carnality or even that which is demonic. In 1 Corinthians 12:10 the gift is described as "the ability to distinguish between spirits." All believers are to question, examine, judge, search into matters

in the appropriate manner. See 1 Corinthians 2:14 and 1 John 4:1-6. Some believers will have discernment in a special sense, thus sharpening the insight of an assembly and on particular occasions might speak up to instruct or warn the church. In contrast with speaking gifts, discernment is more a gift of listening and observing.

In churches where this gift has gone to seed, so to speak, a critical, judgmental cloud chokes the good life of the people; in contrast, the church without this gift functioning is apt to be naive and polluted with hypocrisy and error. Let the balance of 1 Corinthians 13:5-6 prevail, and the motivation will be a delight in the truth.

8. *Mercy*—results in a demonstration of pity and kindness to those in the church who are more miserable and less popular. The exercise of the gift brings an easing of burdens on older ones and help for the handicapped and misfits. This gift is related to that of service or helps, and it shines out especially to those in humiliating or awkward conditions—in other words, the disadvantaged. Romans 12:8 adds an interesting requirement, saying that the mercy must be shown with a cheerful, gracious attitude.

9. *Administration* (or *leading*)—the capability to execute, implement, and coordinate the various functions in a local body of Christ. This spiritual ability maintains unity, order, and harmony so that there can be growth, fruitfulness, and achievement of goals. Churches desperately need those who can visualize goals, organize, and preside, carrying things through to the desired end. Confusion is kept to a minimum in congregations where this gift is recognized and relied upon. See Romans 12:8.

10. *Service* (or *helps*)—the ability to lend a helping hand exactly when and where needed. Properly applied, this gift frees

bogged-down members from practical hindrances so that they have greater freedom to exercise their own gifts effectively. The recipients of this assistance are thereby delivered from embittering burdens and enter happily into their own service. Behind the scenes in every vibrant, happy, growing congregation are those exercising this blessed gift.

11. *Giving*—the capacity to earn and share with wisdom and cheerfulness. Such gifted members manage their own affairs with special wisdom and are enabled thereby to share more largely in the needs of others. On the one hand, they will resist mere emotional appeals, and on the other, be quite sensitive in discovering true needs. This spiritual capability is to be distinguished from the general duty of all Christians to give tithes and offerings for God's work. Study Romans 12:8, 13 and Acts 20:33-35. Notice also the attitude of love required for a proper exercise of this particular gift (1 Cor. 13:3), which results in an overflowing of thanksgiving from many hearts (2 Cor. 9:12).

12. *Healings*—the capability of using Spirit-given faith to foster healing by God's power. God can and does heal today. He might do so with any sickness, regardless of its type or degree of seriousness. God might heal immediately or gradually, with or without medical means. However, God does not always heal (2 Tim. 4:20), and even the apostle himself had to bear his thorn in the flesh. Notice that 1 Corinthians 12:9 speaks of "gifts of healings," using plural terms. Probably this indicates various levels and types of healing ministries as required in the church.

James instructs the sick one to seek help from the elders of the church (James 5:14). This apparently was a private function in the home. Healings at levels deeper than physical will require application of Scripture and prayer. In conclusion, remember that the gift of healings was originally a sign gift but now more appropriately functions for the relief of the members and continues as a special ability to help the church be sound in body, mind, and spirit.

13. *Miracles*—a sign gift predominant in the launching phase of the church. These wonder works were linked with the spread of God's Word and served to confirm his message. Study carefully Romans 15:18-20 and Hebrews 2:3-4.

14. *Tongues*—the gift of languages, known or unknown. It is a sign gift. I will say more about this shortly.

15. *Interpretation*—ability to understand tongues.

Categorizing the Gifts

Spiritual gifts are of three major types. The first five listed above involve a direct use of Scripture. Gifts 6-11 might be called general service gifts. Healings might also be included here, depending on how one defines the gift.

Finally, there are the sign gifts. Some of today's tensions regarding these can be alleviated if the biblical data are carefully inspected. Helpful principles in making such determinations are given in chapter 1. Remember the relation between the five books of history and the twenty-two books of commentary. The sign gifts entered very largely into the launching of the church. Now that Christianity has an established footing in the world and the Scripture is available in written form, we should expect the church to move along in orbit without requiring the same launching equipment. This explains why, as the church developed, the Epistles gave full instruction for the ongoing use of various gifts having to do with the Scripture and general service but did not emphasize the sign gifts.

God's intentions regarding the gifts are revealed to us in the Scriptures. The first five books of the New Testament give the history and outline the events. Miraculous signs were a part of that history. Tongues were a part of the events in the last book of history (i.e., Acts). These narrative books are then followed by twenty-two books of instructions to the churches. In one section of one of the Epistles (1 Corinthians), there is a mention of the problems and concerns of tongues-speaking. Nowhere else is it mentioned, and the church is not given instructions on seeking signs as a part of ongoing church life. For example, when Paul wrote his very complete instructions to the Roman believers, he covered all the essentials of salvation and church life, giving an entire chapter to gifts of the Spirit. Sign gifts are conspicuously absent from Romans 12.

But it should be remembered that whatever a church requires in the way of gifts will be provided by the Head. In the early days of Christianity as the vast worldwide heathendom was being first challenged, God authenticated his tiny minority with signs and wonders. Today Scriptures are fully written and in hand, and the church has a significant place in our world. However, when missionary advances penetrate a deprived, illiterate, and primitive situation that threatens to extinguish the light, certain signs might again occur. The main thing is that God must be sovereign; he will undoubtedly work within the confines of scriptural teaching and the wholesome balance we have discussed among the two divisions of New Testament books.

Scripture also gives warning passages concerning signs and wonders of an evil, counterfeit type that multiply during the final phases of history (e.g., Matt. 24:24; 2 Thess. 2:9-10). Notice in the second reference that the reason for people's calamitous fall is an interest in the signs and wonders rather than precious truth.

Growing a Gifted Assembly

God's pattern for developing a congregation that thrives with the life stimulated and encouraged by operation of the varied spiritual gifts is presented rather clearly in Ephesians 4:11-13. It can be outlined simply as in figure 6.

Figure 6: Diagram of Ephesians 4:11-13

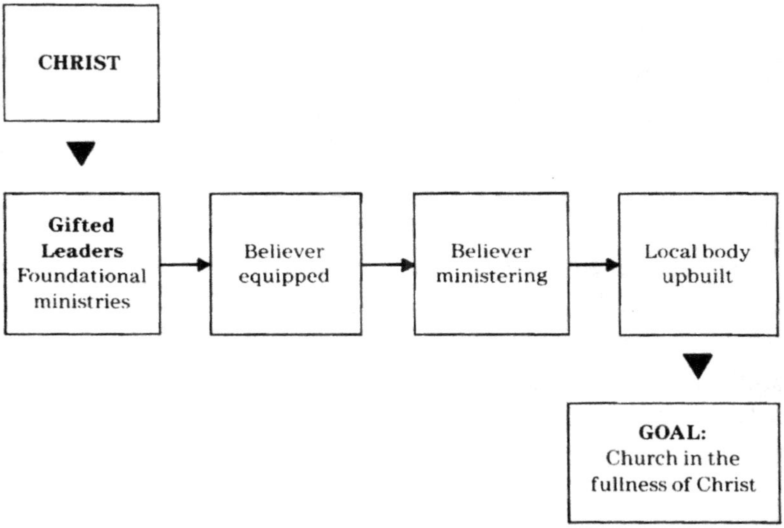

```
┌──────────────┐
│   CHRIST     │
│              │
└──────────────┘
       ▼
┌──────────────┐   ┌──────────────┐   ┌──────────────┐   ┌──────────────┐
│   Gifted     │   │              │   │              │   │              │
│   Leaders    │ → │  Believer    │ → │  Believer    │ → │ Local body   │
│ Foundational │   │  equipped    │   │ ministering  │   │  upbuilt     │
│  ministries  │   │              │   │              │   │              │
└──────────────┘   └──────────────┘   └──────────────┘   └──────────────┘
                                                                 ▼
                                                        ┌──────────────┐
                                                        │   GOAL:      │
                                                        │ Church in the│
                                                        │ fullness of Christ│
                                                        └──────────────┘
```

The large steps for growing a gifted assembly might be stated as follows:

1. Structuring along biblical lines involving all the members and their gifts.
2. Giving instructions regarding the gifts—both in regular preaching and teaching and in special training sessions.
3. Offering practical assistance to discover and use gifts. Here are the directions which I have used in helping believers become more settled as to what their spiritual capabilities really are:
    a. Study and meditate on pertinent Scripture.

b. Pray, asking God for understanding, divine enablement, and the filling of the Holy Spirit.

c. Serve in various capacities, exposing yourself to God and his fields of ministry.

d. Seek the counsel and confirmation of fellow believers.

Now allow me to make a few concluding observations. First, each member should with confident anticipation discover his or her own gifts and then move to assist others in the same process. Remember also that spiritual gifts may appear singly, but usually an individual will possess his or her own particular pattern of abilities.

Next, the congregation itself must be edified to the place where they fully accept their own leaders and ministering ones. As we have shown, *all* will have gifts to serve, and *some* will in addition hold office. Let the *some* remember the *all*, and let the *all* respect the *some*.

The truly maturing, edified church will then be receptive to its own leadership and ministries and will continue diligently developing both. As Romans 1:11-12 suggests, the benefit of gifted ministry is mutual, that is, both giving and receiving.

Attitudes and dispositions seen during the exercises of spiritual gifts are very important. Reading Romans 12, 1 Corinthians 12–14, and other related texts shows how ruinous carnality is to the proper exercise of the gifts. Let there be no antagonism, jealousy, inferiority, pride, or rivalries.

Finally, consider what potential (often unrealized) is suggested by statements like the following: "Now to each one the manifestation of the Spirit is given for the common good. . . . All these are the work of one and the same Spirit, and he gives them to each one, just as he determines" (1 Cor. 12:7, 11). However, we do not see God forcing this promised fullness into a church's life. Instead, divine sovereignty awaits human concurrence. This means that God requires believers to take some such steps as we have proposed toward his supply of grace, and then the gifts will appear and develop.

Appendix 3

A Transitional Structure

The listing below is intended to provoke fresh thoughts about the church's structure and preparation for ministry. Notice that the eldership has responsibility for the spiritual life of the church and its various ministries; the deacons, however, share in leading important spiritual ministries and have charge of much of the mechanical operation of the church.

Notice further that elders and deacons share together in certain functions of Christian education and missions. Probably those key committees would be led by two different elders. Then certain vital functions of each committee would be reported to, and supervised by, elders, whereas other such functions would be reported to the deacons.

Members of the committees would be chosen from the church at large. Figure 7 is intended only to propose ideas for moving the leaders of the church into positions where they can serve the church in a more biblical and effective manner and to provoke fresh thoughts about the church's structure and preparation for ministry.

Figure 7: A Transitional Structure

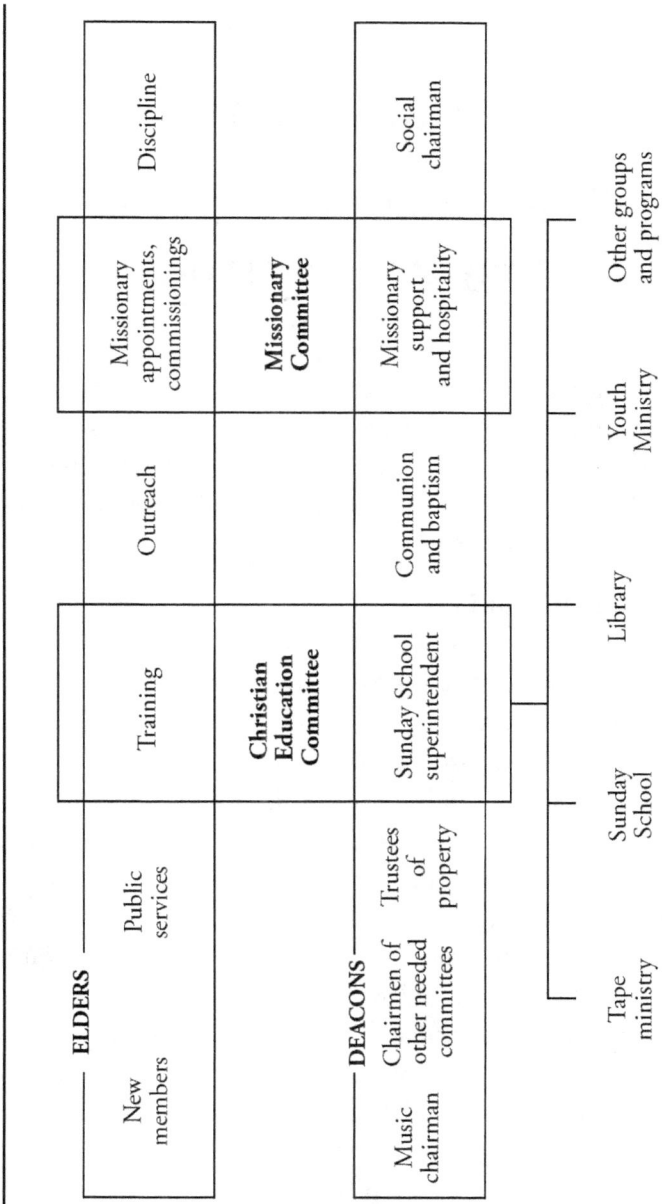

Appendix 4

Suggestions for a Day of Prayer and Fasting

An extended time of praying and fasting sounds very imposing to those who have not experienced it. Let us remove some of the questions surrounding the subject. Whether for an individual, a team of leaders, or the entire church family, the objectives are likely to be one or more of a few basic types.

Purposes of Days of Prayer

1. Deepening communion with the Lord. Somewhat like a married couple might go away for a time of reflection and renewing their love vows, so our life with God needs periods when we retire to refresh our love for him.

2. Discovering God's will. This might involve simply making a specific decision, or it might concern one's entire life-direction or perhaps whether to enter a new ministry and, if so, how to accomplish it.

3. Gaining new power in service. Fruitfulness is related to prayer (John 14:12-14; 15:7-8, 16).

4. Growing in personal holiness. Just as those who spend time in the sun show it upon their faces, so it is with those who take longer periods in God's presence. A day of prayer is also an ideal time for breaking with any sin that has brought defeat into the life. God is ready with help (Heb. 4:16).

5. Making intercession. Great is the privilege of spending time in prayer for other persons and their needs or even for one's own problems.

A Word about Fasting

Why fast? Through this added discipline, one's entire being is quieted and concentration made easier. All concern about the time being invested, anxiety over business, and even the matter of eating must be set aside. Fasting does in no way earn merit points with God, but it does assist in giving full attention to the Lord himself and his Word.

At first, slight headaches or other complaints from the stomach might trouble a bit. These difficulties usually subside in time. During longer fasts—stretching beyond a day in length—hunger and other distresses tend to disappear as one persists, and sharpening of the mental faculties is noticeable.

Those who are just beginning this practice will probably do well to undertake a more limited fast through a single meal or portion of a day. This may be done with or without liquids, since the fast is for a short period. Determine these details ahead of time. Remember that the main issue at hand is not the fasting itself but communion with God through prayer.

Procedure for a Brief Personal Fasting and Prayer Time

Everything begins the night before. Dedicate the approaching night of rest and the coming special day to God in prayer. Lay out your plans for the day. Decide whether or not you shall drink water or any juices. Place essential equipment at the selected place for your praying. Have at hand a good Bible translation or two and perhaps a hymnbook to aid in worship. You will need a supply of notepaper and a pen to record new insights and any particular instruction received from God as you pray and search through Scripture. Now retire early, commending yourself into the Lord's hands.

Next morning arise early, and after a quick wake-up shower get directly to your place of prayer. Do not break the fast. Begin by reading aloud on your knees a worship psalm such as 145. Perhaps take time to list descriptions of God you see there or in other psalms. Then worship our Lord for each attribute you have listed.

I would urge you early in your day to invest time in taking spiritual inventory. Some of the middle chapters in Proverbs are a great help in searching every area of life and practice. As failures, weaknesses, and oversights are brought to mind by the Holy Spirit using the Word, directly confess each sin and claim the blood of Christ for cleansing. Make it a time of full confession and restoration.

Undoubtedly a major part of your time should be spent in reading and praying through Scripture books. Decide whether to use James, Peter's epistles, a Gospel, Philippians, Isaiah, or some other book or books. God will help you make the most appropriate selection. As you come to a truth that particularly stands out to your mind, pause for very deliberate prayer concerning it. Perhaps you will want to make notes summarizing what you have learned.

Remember to change positions as often as necessary, sometimes kneeling, perhaps with the Bible and notes open before you, and at other times standing in order to keep alert.

Intensive intercession will be possible at such time. Cover in detail all the matters for which you have set aside the day. Also allow the Holy Spirit to lay other burdens upon you.

Likely, a brief fast will extend no more than through the noon hour. At some point then during the afternoon, you will perhaps break the fast and have a light lunch—unless, of course, you have determined to continue until the dinner hour. Always remember that the longer the fast, the lighter should be your first intake of nourishment. Heavy eating and excited activities can rob you of the day's benefits. Therefore it is important to guard all that you have gained by continued emphasis on prayer over the next day or two. Ask God for special protection against Satan and any debilitating emotional depression.

Special Suggestions for Public Days of Prayer and Fasting

An outline for public prayer and fasting might be very similar to that used by an individual in private. Here is a useful outline:

1. Opening prayers of dedication.
2. Inspirational singing.
3. Worship time—various uses of Scripture, prayer, singing, spiritual inventory, and intercession. This should be done alone, using assigned chapters in Proverbs and other texts such as Psalm 51 and 1 John 1:7. Perhaps after 20 or at most 30 minutes, everyone should re-gather for continuing public prayer.
4. United devotion to the main issue at hand—for example, outreach, church renewal, or the like. Any further information to be presented should be done quickly and efficiently so that prayer can be dominant.
5. After brief united prayer, division into smaller groups for a more intensive time of intercession.
6. Re-gathering for testimonies and/or sharing of personal burdens.
7. Final period of fresh dedication by all; individuals who are willing, lead in public prayer. Here the church literally presents itself to the Head for a new and deeper ministry. Blessings will follow.

Suggested Printed Materials

Following are three samples of actual printed material I have used in past ministry. First, here is a copy of an announcement that appeared in the Sunday bulletin just prior to the day of prayer:

Day of Prayer (and Fasting) Sat., 9 a.m.–Noon

Here's how:

> Begin Friday night—retire early after special prayer, dedicating the night's rest and day of prayer.
>
> *If you choose to fast*—decide whether with or without liquids. Rise early Saturday a.m. and do not break the fast, but get right to prayer and Scripture.
>
> *Be at church by 9 a.m.* We will have varying periods of worship, heart-searching, and intercession. Our aim will be to reconsecrate ourselves to God and see new depth and progress in the church.

Note the special insert in today's bulletin.

Next is given the simultaneous bulletin insert that prepared the people for this very searching experience:

Suggestions for Saturday Day of Prayer

> Meditate on Psalm 86. Make a list of all items for praise you see—descriptions of God and his works. Praise him for each.
>
> Must praying always be a pleasant experience? See Luke 22:39-46.
>
> What is the danger of giving up prayer? v. 46
>
> What causes us to go this way? (See also Matt. 26:41.)
>
> In this connection, meditate on Peter's good intentions and yet sad failure, Luke 22:31-34, 54-62. What was the basic cause?
>
> Continuing the lessons about our sinful weakness in Matt.

142

26:41, read carefully Rom. 8:1-14. Rejoice in the facts of vv. 9 and 10. Then make a claim on what v. 13 suggests. Now you are ready for vv. 14 to 26 and 27: AMEN!

With praise and thanksgiving pray over, phrase by phrase, verses 31-39 of Romans 8.

After getting a hold on this higher ground, bring out into the light your own deepest troubles, sins, burdens. Now, with firm faith claim, even out loud, v. 37; repeat it until faith revives.

It is time to praise God, from whom all blessings flow.

Requests for Prayer (Note John 14:13-14; James 5:16)

That the Holy Spirit will unify all our hearts in true love.

That each believer will be lifted to a new level of "care one for another" (1 Cor. 12:25).

That there will be greater freedom in all our services as we worship together— especially in times of singing and sharing of testimonies and prayer.

That our homes will be filled with new love and unity, with new interest in family worship and prayer for one another.

That hidden defeats in many lives will be brought out into the light of surrender to our Lord, even this very day, and that where needed, apologies will be given and all wrongs made right—according to Matt. 5:23-24.

Pray for every believer you know of who is fallen, troubled, or out of fellowship with God and man.

Now, reach out in prayer to unsaved individuals as the Lord lays them on your heart.

Mention before God each missionary you know.

Walk by faith over the continents and stand with them in prayer.

143

Finally, the "personal sheet" below is a helpful guide for one attempting a private day of prayer.

Personal Sheet

Have the eyes of your heart been seeing new spiritual truths lately?

Pray and read Luke 10:38-42.

After this first thoughtful reading, go through again, answering the following:

v. 39

- Have you been doing this regularly? Does the Holy Spirit make Scripture and prayer this real to you?

vv. 40-41

- Are you "troubled about many things?" Are circumstances, busyness, tensions keeping you from the Lord? (Even things not evil in themselves are sinful if they separate us from Christ.)

- Are there any unforsaken sins wracking conscience or deadening your heart and grieving God?

- Note carefully what is the one truly *needful* thing—the "good part" that Mary chose. Martha missed it. Have you?

Suggested Order for a Time of Prayer:

1. *Period of definite and thorough confession regarding:*
   Tensions in personal life, home, business
   Any continuing sin keeping nerves raw and spiritual pulse and love low (Talk it over with God, calling the sin by name.)
   Neglect of personal devotion and love for the Lord and his Word

144

Known failures in home and family relationships

2. *Period of praise and thanks that his love continues*
   For the blood of Christ, 1 John 1:7
   That all is right and restored—even bettered! Amen. Praise
   God.
   Worship God using Psalm 100.

3. *Period of rededication*
   Adapt King David's strong affirmations to your life using
   Psalm 101.
   Say, "The Lord helping me, *I will!*"

Appendix 5

Leadership Authority and the Integrity of the Congregation

In some church fellowships, local congregations govern by legal votes on many items. A loss of leadership initiative and authority sometimes results. If, however, a fellowship grants its leaders a considerable authority and expects them to lead in a strong manner, it will be necessary to maintain watch over the integrity of the congregational responsibilities.

A study of Acts 6:1-7 shows the early Christian body to be active in this instance of selecting members to direct a certain project. These newly appointed leaders then carried out their responsibility—perhaps reporting to the congregation or to the apostles.

How does the body act officially? Patient instruction can lead to unanimous action. Unanimity can be maintained if those with minority or contrary opinions are given definite opportunity (a stated number of days) to explain their reservations. During the period of deliberation and consultation, if members of the minority opinion provide substantial grounds for their position, the matter should be rethought and presented in a revised form. But if those in the minority are unable to give further information, they should be encouraged to see the position of the leaders and the majority of the congregation. In cases where there is obstinacy and unwillingness either to provide new light and insight from their points of view or to receive new information from others, their opinions must be set aside, at least for the issue at hand. Therefore, all persons with contrary opinions must be prayerfully listened to and everything held in abeyance as long as there is openness and it appears that continuing exchange is helpful.

These proceedings are sometimes wonderfully facilitated when there is a day of fasting and prayer scheduled in connection with crucial issues. (See appendix 4.) Along the way, it is not unspiritual to employ signed ballots or response sheets or to conduct a "sense vote" to see how the congregation is being led in certain matters. These procedures would not need to be considered as legally binding.

Selecting and Installing Officers

Selection of new leaders should involve both the church body and the present leaders. The wholesome spiritual procedures seen in Scripture should be recognized as ideals for the local assembly. Rash, disturbing action to change things is uncalled for.

In many cases a significant leadership position can be filled in such a way as to satisfy both the deeper spiritual principles as well as any constitutional requirements in that particular communion. Before the traditional balloting procedure is set in motion, perhaps a period of prayerful deliberation could be engaged in by the whole fellowship. Next, one of two procedures could be chosen: The congregation could present all its suggested names to the elders, thereby saying, Here are the ones who are acceptable to us; you pray and choose which of these shall perform the duties in office. Or the elders could present nominations to the church body. In such a case the leaders would make arrangements for members to voice their approval of the ones considered best for the positions. Written response might be asked for—or at least provisions made for answering questions and hearing negative reactions.

Again, every opposing voice can be fully listened to in this way. If opposition proves substantial and cannot be satisfied, then such a person should not be presented for the office.

When patiently followed, this procedure promotes healthy unanimity. The congregation will need preparation, of course. Principles covered in chapter 4 come into play at this point.

Appendix 6

How You Can Have Family Bible Reading and Prayer

Dear Reader,

Years of thought and experience are behind the suggestions that follow. My earnest prayer is that this tool will help many to hold regular, meaningful family worship of our God and Savior—going through the Bible together. God bless you as you put it into practice!

Pastor Burchett

Beginning and Continuing

Best is not to decide each day to have Bible and prayer. Rather, decide now to have Bible and prayer each day. Notice the difference. Make one decision and stick by it.

My instructions are addressed to families. However, I wish to include all singles—those living alone or those with others in the same dwelling. These too should undertake this daily fellowship. Where this is not possible, then I strongly urge each one to follow the plan alone.

Family relationships and individual lives will be purified by Scripture truth, like a regular washing of the soul. God's teachings give support to right living. In this way, *God is present daily!*

Steps toward Meaningful Family Worship

1. Agreement of parents to have family worship is worth great effort. The ideal is for Dad to take initiative as leader, using the others. God will, of course, bless the mother who, after waiting for Dad, must alone plan the time and guide the children in worship.

2. Set a definite time when the family can be together. (Just after supper hour is ideal. It is surely worth setting the meal schedule to fit this in before evening responsibilities.)

3. Expect difficulties. Do not quit. Humbly keep trying. If needed, administer firm discipline afterward, or on occasion interrupt briefly to care for misbehavior. However, strive for cheerful, quiet cooperation. As a regular daily pattern, train babies to be still, apart from worship time.

4. Keep it brief and bright, 10 to 20 minutes. Avoid long, tiring lectures or trying to cover too much. Tomorrow will come! In emergencies, greatly abbreviate rather than eliminate. Here is one shortened form: Share a key thought, all stand in circle for prayer holding hands while one leads. Or even start discussion during the meal, when pressed for time.

5. Prepare briefly in advance. Glance over the next Bible portion to be covered. Remember the main aim is to cover the Bible itself, but the Bible in storybook form will help tiny youngsters get hold of important history faster. However, even younger children need to hear Bible language daily. Read it and tell it, both.

6. Vary the method of covering each Bible portion. Try the following, changing each week:

   a. One person read entire portion—taking turns night by night.

   b. Have each person in the circle read one or several verses.

(Or in the case of very small children, let them take their turn, too, by repeating the words after you as you read phrase by phrase.)

c. If the day's Scripture section is a very long, single episode, prepare to tell the story briefly, having all read key verses. (This takes but a few moments of advance preparation.)

d. Employ the family members in turn as leaders. Coach them in advance to know leading points, questions, ideas of approach.

e. Assignments: Map study, noticing areas being studied; questions and truths bearing on the text; terms (Bible dictionary); related Scriptures.

7. Lead brief discussion and/or question time. Frequent questions interspersed in a story will stimulate the interest of the very young. Aim questions at facts just read and also to see if all get the meaning and application to their lives. (Here parents should humbly share from their heart, too.) "What blessing or lesson is here for you?" "Explain verse ___." "What did Jesus do/ say here?" "What does this teach us about the Lord?" "Are we ever guilty of this?" "How?" "Are there things we sometimes try to hide?" "What are *your* main problems?"

8. Time of prayer. Suggested subjects: define home needs, needs of each other and of others, salvation of friends, neighbors, relatives. Sometimes take special requests from each one. Remember our various missionaries—perhaps one for an entire week. Hold to the great aim of prayer: real praise and thanks. Each worship time should raise the family's view of God himself and *his* workings on earth. Pray around the circle. Or by ages; or select certain ones to lead. Sometimes sit, another time stand, or kneel. (Don't avoid this for comfort's sake.) Once in a while, use the Lord's Prayer in unison to close or open a prayer period.

Note: A moment of help to younger children before kneeling is time well spent. Reflect on a lesson for their life in the Bible portion just covered. Say, "You can pray (ask, thank) about that." Or "What is one special blessing you can thank God for this evening?" Or a sentence of help regarding the missionary needing prayer. For the very young, you will want to prepare even their way of saying their brief prayer. Soon they will gather more ideas of their own in spontaneous praying.

9. Other worship activities. (Must be done quickly as a bright worship aid.) Hymn singing. Use a verse or two of a familiar hymn or chorus before prayer or as you open worship. Try memorizing a good hymn. Purchase your own hymnals, matching those in church. Memorize Scripture verses together. Act out the Bible story.

10. Always invite any guests to sit with you. Never omit devotions or apologize. Simply say, "We are so glad you are with us now because each evening we have a brief family time with the Bible." Either include the visitor in the circle of reading or ask only the children to read and you close with any discussion and prayer. If the guests are believers, it will be an added blessing to all if they share more fully.

11. Further thoughts: Once in a while, deliberately change the time and place. For example, on a Saturday try family worship in the morning, and move everyone's private morning devotions to the evening. Sunday afternoon have worship outdoors or around the fireplace, or enlarge the activity to include a full service at home. Tie the worship in with various good family times. Make it a part of highlight occasions. Parents should not allow complaining or contesting for place in worship time The parent should always keep the initiative, deciding how each session shall be handled. Keep it alive and interesting.

Appendix 7

Practical Help for Parents Whose Child Comes to Personal Faith in Christ

The following paragraphs were prepared as a help for parents in raising their children as followers of Christ.]

When a child expresses his or her faith in Jesus Christ, there will be signs of a new spiritual life that will need careful cultivation. Giving one's allegiance to Christ forever is a big step. Young people can make such a step, but they will need their parents' help.

The church stands ready to assist, providing literature and counsel. However, the Bible makes it clear that children have been committed to their *parents*. How discouraging it is when the church alone does the teaching! Children who are merely church-taught and not home-taught almost invariable fall away.

A child must have a Christian home. We are asking you to take the initiative and the responsibility before God to prepare your child—to reach your child in the way of God.

"Is my child too young?"
This is often asked. It really is not simply a matter of age. Often it is a matter of the will. Is your child ready and willing to follow

Christ? Are you, the parent, willing to take your God-given responsibility?

If the child does not desire—or is not permitted—to share in the simple schedule of weekly services, then this ought to be considered before applying for church membership. Outside the Lord's Day itself, the schedule might include a midweek service of prayer, fellowship, and testimony time. Young people need to hear from other Christians so that they can be well-rounded and instructed. Any hesitation on attendance at services should be settled first.

"How may I help?"

Nothing strikes deeper—for good or bad—into a youngster's heart than the everyday example of the parent. Next, direct and daily instruction using any literature provided by the church will be invaluable. In addition, surrounding the child with the atmosphere of Christian home worship will keep him or her on the way. Daily family devotions need not be long and perhaps can be done just after supper or at some convenient, regular time. Brief, earnest prayers and a short passage from a book of the Bible will get you under way.

Parents who have children seeking to live Christian lives must beware of discouraging them. When they fail and sin and require rebuke and punishment, it ought to be done in a proper manner. Repeated remarks such as, "You don't act like a Christian!" are apt to be fatally discouraging. It is true that they need to be reminded that God sees *all* and that their life may be disappointing him. However, this ought never be done in the heat of the moment but later—perhaps after appropriate punishment has been administered. Lovingly and prayerfully encourage them to seek the Lord's forgiveness and trust the Spirit to help them in the future.

It would be an excellent thing to help them establish their *own* devotional life of private prayer and Bible reading.

No doubt the subject of their baptism will come up. As we have already pointed out, if they are encouraged to lead a regular church life, then this ought to be considered soon. As they apply, you can help them prepare by following through on the matters discussed above. In addition, see that they are acquainted with at least one or two of the elders or deacons and recognize some of the other officers. Make sure, too, that the pastor or shepherd knows your child by name.

Finally, I urge you to keep this sheet for repeated review and checkup in the future. (A lot of ground is covered here!) Perhaps fold it and place it in your Bible.

Train up a child in the way he should go:
and when he is old, he will not depart from it.
(Prov. 22:6).

Appendix 8

Evangelism and Prayer

Prayer has an absolutely essential relationship to everything having to do with evangelism. Apart from prayer, there is no true evangelism. Indeed, the effectiveness of the one depends on the other.

Preparing the ground, sowing the seed, struggling against evil spiritual forces, opening the understanding of the unbeliever, sustaining the new believer in the way—all depends upon prayer. The fruit comes only in response to earnest prayer. Study carefully such passages as John 15:7-8, 16; Col. 4:2-5, and Luke 11:1-22, where Jesus' teaching on perseverance in prayer should be related to that on the binding of the strong man and freeing souls from his control.

Much can be learned from our Lord's parable of the seed and sower. Turn to Luke 8:4-15. Discover the problems facing the evangelist, or seed-sower. Make a written list of all the difficulties you see described. All the forces or conditions that prevent production of fruit must be confronted in intercessory prayer.

Endlessly throwing seed into unprepared soil is not the way. Much prayer before giving out the Word, and continuance in prayer thereafter, is urgently important.

One further matter needs highlighting. Most of the training and emphasis on evangelism aims at overcoming the barrier between the person who witnesses and the unbeliever who hears.

There is indeed somewhat of a communication gap there, but that is not the great problem. When a spokesman speaks in God's name, the chasm is not simply person to person, but the gulf existing between wayward man and the holy God must be overcome. Prayer helps bridge across.

Appendix 9

Doctrines and Practices—a Composite of the Christian Life

A discipler of others would do well to compile a list of all the points essential to the Christian faith and practice and then make frequent reference to the list. If the compilation embraces the key, broad truths of Christian doctrine and basic areas of responsibility, it will then represent a composite of vital Christianity.

The checklists reproduced on the following page are taken from the section "The Leader's Preparation" in my personal edification manual, *Spiritual Life Studies*. The doctrines should each be touched on repeatedly and deepened in the understanding, while appealing for appropriate response in the practices listed.

Doctrines

___ The person of Christ
___ The death of Christ
___ The Trinity
___ The doctrine of sin
___ The new birth
___ The humanity of Christ
___ Victorious living
___ Scripture
___ Satisfaction in Christ's provisions
___ Return of Christ and the life to come
___ Person and ministries of the Holy Spirit
___ Deity of Christ
___ Activity of Satan
___ Afflictions and trial
___ Prayer in Jesus' name
___ Our identity with Christ
___ Principles of spiritual warfare
___ The resurrection of Christ
___ Release from sin's penalty and relief from its power
___ The transformed life

Practices

___ Witnessing
___ Assurance of Salvation
___ Confession of sin
___ Personal worship
___ Repentance and laying aside of sin habits
___ Daily Bible reading
___ Dedication to service
___ Standing against opposition
___ Ministry to others
___ Being Spirit-filled
___ Godly standards
___ Spiritual warfare
___ Deeper prayer life
___ Self-denial
___ Abiding in Christ
___ Fruit-bearing
___ Family life
___ Baptism
___ Use of spiritual gifts

Appendix 10

Beginning a Daughter Church

One church I am very familiar with followed a growth pattern summarized in these nine steps:

1. Men of a target area met for Saturday morning prayer. Such a weekly gathering had long been a tradition at the main church. But now these men were being encouraged to pray and deliberate separately in their own locale.

2. All leaders agreed as to what would be counted as acceptable evidences of the Spirit's leading toward formation of another church fellowship. It was decided that the time would be considered ripe when believers in the new fellowship and at the central congregation were in agreement that adequate leadership existed in the young work and definite evangelistic results were issuing from the new fellowship itself. It was also agreed to begin looking early for confirming evidence of an outgrowth from the new work. Thus, as the nucleus became a distinct cell, it would already be in the process of multiplication.

3. An agenda of services was developed, beginning with weekly prayer meetings in the area. Three of these weekly meetings each month were scheduled in various homes, while the other one or two were in rented facilities. Evening services followed next. After these meetings were established and growing, morning services would be scheduled at some later time.

4. Leaders of the embryonic fellowship gradually took over

more responsibilities. All the while, they continued to share official duties at the main church, so that every move was fully coordinated and agreed on.

5. Elders and deacons were selected and commissioned.

6. Members from the main church were dismissed to legally form the new body.

7. The process of disengaging administrative and financial matters was completed.

8. Vital fellowship was continued between the old and new groups. Monthly meetings were scheduled, usually prayer services—in rented facilities when the main church auditorium became too small for both groups.

9. A senior pastor of the central body remained on call and available for counsel and continued to have a spiritual relationship with the elders of the new assembly, though the pastor in no sense has any ruling authority.

Several very large purposes are realized by expanding in the above manner. First of all, it makes a center for fellowship more available for believers in their own immediate area. New leaders are developed as they are forced into greater roles of responsibility. More believers are involved in diversified ministries. Finally, the gospel light shines more intensely in each area when a congregation meets there. Contact with homes in the various residential sections and on school campuses or in places of business is much more direct and meaningful when a congregation concentrates its evangelistic efforts closer at home.

The deliberateness of this approach keeps the infant church in the womb until viability is certain. Miscarriages are thus prevented.

A peculiar problem sometimes faced concerns mis-understandings by other churches already existing in the new areas of outgrowth. A possible solution would be for the main church pastor to establish a bond of fellowship with the pastor serving nearest the target area. Interaction with him in prayer meetings or services might be arranged. This could be followed by developing relationship between the congregations until God indicated what further course of action should be taken. If there is a definite quickening and unity of fellowship, then the whole enterprise can be reshaped and the main church pour its outlying strengths into that church or churches already existing.

If, however, there is a restrained spirit and no indication of encouraging new life in those existing churches, then the main church would be free to seek further direction from God regarding its own independent expansion.

In conclusion, keep in mind three important principles when considering cell-type expansion of a local church:

1. Depend on free cooperation of all members living in the new area. Do not unduly press them to join the outgrowth venture.

2. During the protracted transition period, continue a common body of elders so as to assure deep communication and to maintain spiritual unity.

3. Pace the disengagement with the segment's development as a living nucleus, looking for specific evidences of growing autonomy.

Appendix 11

Biblical Support—the Earliest Churches in Homes

The biblical expression "the church that meets in their house" (Rom. 16:5), referring here to the residence of Priscilla and Aquila, means that this couple hosted an identifiable segment of the larger church at Rome. Evidence seems to indicate that a very substantial company of elders led the church, but no evidence exists from the first century of a building large enough to accommodate the sizable congregation gathered from the whole city. Did not the church at Rome (as well as larger city congregations elsewhere) meet more often in neighborhood churches and then, when possible, gather for whole-church meetings either in rented quarters or outdoors?

Early house churches, as replicas of the whole city church, were ideally pastored by elders. Study Romans 16:3-5, 1 Corinthians 16:19, Colossians 4:15-16, and Philemon 1-2.

—Taken from my book *Bringing Christ Back*, 195-96

Appendix 12

Next Steps in Forming Churches in the Home

The following is a pastoral letter I sent to a main church that was moving toward forming churches in members' homes.

Much visitation has already taken place by team members among their flocks. As the contacts continue, they now can relate somewhat to the church-in-the-home emphasis getting underway.

Each flock must be subdivided into house churches. It is not our objective to build a large, comfortable home Bible study or prayer fellowship in each area. Rather, we should aim at multiplying gatherings of 12 to 25, all under capable leadership.

Members of several families, along with singles, will form these basic assemblies. Children will be included from the outset, since it is a church, not simply an adult meeting. (See appendix 7, where I detail a plan for caring for the very young children.)

Hopefully, each house church will grow and divide into other fellowships. Unless all are taught this vision from the outset, there will be considerable resistance to it. The idea is to make centers of worship available to as many people as possible, right where they live.

Obviously, we can't dictate to folks exactly where they will align themselves in worship. But we can lay down the challenge of permeating our entire area with happy, victorious, growing families of families. All of us can grow and change in the light of such a vision.

Finding a place to meet will be important, but the real issue will be leadership, which is crucial for growth and multiplication. Each believer must be challenged to find out what his or her spiritual strengths and gifts really are.

I present the alliteration GOTHS to make it easier to remember what the beginning, basic ministries are for the house churches. I list them here, giving a few comments with each one. (As time goes on, much training should be given to the people doing each of these ministries.)

GATHERERS

People do not naturally and easily become participants in home meetings. They must be led into it by someone they respond to who has what I refer to as the "gift of gathering." Early on, we must discover these warm and gregarious people.

ORGANIZERS

Home gatherings have a way of going to seed rather quickly if someone is not caring for orderliness. This gift is important to keep the small gatherings functioning in a way that is effective and meeting the needs of everyone.

Somehow it is of the nature of home gatherings for the informality to deteriorate into a type of disorganized discussions and directionless fellowship. For this reason, dependable time frames of beginning and ending the meetings need to be established.

A key issue in developing gifts is that those who are leaders must realize that no one person has all the gifts; each must learn to relax on the wings of other people's strengths. Do not try to lead and run the show in an area where you are not spiritually equipped.

TEACHERS

Not everyone with a gift of gab is a good teacher. Indeed, some teach in a very fluent manner, but nothing happens in the hearers' lives. Do they have an anointed gift of teaching or not? Real fruit comes only when God's calling and equipment are in the life. A spiritually gifted teacher can make truth clear and useful in the lives of other believers.

HOSTS

We must find people who have not only space in their homes but who have hearts large enough to make others comfortable in their fellowship. Apart from this gift, many who gather will feel an oppressive restraint or timidity in interacting with one another. It is important that the children be relaxed and happy without being indulged.

Sufficient discipline and control is possible without offense in an atmosphere of relaxed, cheerful fellowship. It is of the nature of small fellowships to quickly move upward or else quickly go downhill.

SHEPHERDS

These men are given in answer to prayer. They have the pastoring gift that each flock needs. They do not necessarily present themselves as the "top dog." They work a lot behind the scenes, but they are continually evaluating and noticing how things are going. Their eye is particularly upon the hearts and inner responses of the believers in their flock. They will make certain that the design of fellowship and relationships in their group is the way it ought to be.

Some of these shepherds will be elders already. Others will be recognized later on as having qualifications of elder, or overseer. In conjunction with this evidence right from the field of service, some shepherds will be added to the congregational board of elders. The place of biblically ordered oversight of these home gatherings is what makes this approach distinct from many of the small-group plans seen around the country today.

Looking again at the five basic ministries, let me point out that one person might serve in two or three of these capacities at the same time. This might not be the ideal, but it will be necessary on most occasions. The main thing is to get all the bases covered.

Launching numbers of churches in the homes at the same time is so humanly impossible that it drives us to Matt. 19:26, "With man this is impossible, but with God all things are possible." It simply will not happen if God does not help us; therefore, we must pray persistently. God wants each one to feel totally responsible, as if everything will stand or fall according to his or her faithfulness in prayer and service.

Now, what is going to take place in a home meeting?

First, there will be the period of welcome, greeting, and fellowship as people gather. This must not go on indeterminably but will have definite boundaries to it. The main meeting must begin at the appointed time, even though everyone will appear to be having a good time. More careful reflection afterward will show that deterioration sets in rather quickly, and the high goals of the fellowship will be lost unless there is a proper measure of order. In addition, it should be remembered that not all people are the same. Many place a high priority on value of time and are more disciplined. These must not be needlessly offended by ragged meetings.

Then these meetings will include Bible study. I suggest

beginning with the Book of Mark. Everyone should be reading this gospel in preparation. The teacher must choose the portion of Scripture he plans to cover. This might be an event or two and/or a parable or teaching by Jesus. Have this read and briefly summarize it so that all are equally aware of the text. Next the teacher will have in mind two or three main teaching points out of the section of Scripture. A teaching point is simply a truth that is developed from the text by using questions, discussion, and teaching. Application to life will be next. The aim of Bible study is not simply to clog heads with more data but to get response in life. Always ask, What impact should this lesson have on each of us here in this room?

Prayer time will be an essential whenever the church meets in the homes. People will want to pray over what they have studied and learned from Scripture. And there will be many real situations in their own lives that can be shared, giving the group the delightful opportunity to share in mutual support.

Without a doubt, believers are generally hungering for deeper relationships with others. Through home meetings, God can enrich each believer's life for the good of the others, as Scripture plainly teaches (1 Cor. 12:7). Just as individual devotions of prayer and Scripture must forever be a daily mark in the believer's life, so fellowship with others in Scripture and prayer must be a regular experience. This latter benefit is not fully realized by looking toward a public platform "up front."

When one person bares a personal need, then others who are present with their spiritual baskets full of good things will meet that need. As folks become more and more open to give and receive help, the matter of discretion will become important. Here the shepherd will have to be alert and see that indiscretions do not develop.

Early in our experience it should be clear that there will be no exalted platforms in the home gatherings. These meetings will not invite shining lights and stars to perform. There will be leadership, however, but not the kind that exalts someone "up front." However, the meetings must not be one grand puddle of unpreparedness in a patented equality. Domination by personalities should be strongly discouraged. However, if adequate emphasis is placed on fruit-bearing outreach, and growth with a view to dividing and beginning new house churches, that "bleeding" experience will tend to prune self-centeredness and keep us healthy and balanced.

Now a word about children in the home meetings. A church in the home is a family affair. Children are a vital part of it and should be made to feel that. What about disruption and discipline problems? There are ways to minimize problems of this kind and at the same time have the blessing of whole families.

First, the meetings must be so interesting and real that even youngsters will be captivated. Infants and less manageable youngsters will be cared for in a separate room. (The mothers will have to take turns watching them.) As parents grow and gain more skill in managing their children, they will be able to have them in the main meeting for longer periods of time. Because the meetings are informal, a parent might stand in the doorway with their little one and then, if the child becomes quiet, return to the meeting. Or if the child continues to be restless, he or she could be taken to the other room. This kind of interaction between families is wholesome and stimulates real growth in all our lives.

Many words could be written about the value this experience has for children and young people. Teenagers, for example, who share regularly in this kind of life, will gain a new respect for their own mothers and dads and other men and women, as the adults use their spiritual gifts in earnest ministry in these close-up relationships.

May God grant us this rich experience!

Appendix 13

Missionary Principles of Outreach

The following letter was written by a faithful missionary wife and raises crucial issues about evangelism:

We have been encouraged with the group here. There are signs of growth. Some are sharing responsibilities with us. N——, one of our young men, attended the Leadership Training School held in the K—— area in Feb. Now he is sharing some of the things he learned from the Book of Revelation. Some of the men have become more serious in their personal lives and witness and also have a more victorious attitude rather than defeat. The Lord is answering prayer and we thank those of you who have prayed. C—— is going through Ephesians on Sunday mornings and is finishing up individual studies with some of the men using the Gospel of John. I am still teaching reading to the women who are interested. This has been (and still is) very difficult for them. I am working on a series of lessons I hope to start in September with the children in our group.

We still need to know the Lord's mind for the village of D—— (there are two Christians there), and also for B——, where there are 15 or so teenagers who profess Christ but are sadly lacking in teaching.

As the need here appears greater and we sense our own inability to meet it, the Lord's promises shine brighter! "The Lord will open the heavens, the storehouse of his bounty" (Deut. 28:12).

And here is a portion of my reply:

> Regarding your mention of developments in D——, B——, and outlying spots, I felt the urge to write, sharing some insights I think are from God. Here is a law: When you *properly* divide a man's territory of ministry, you increase his effectiveness in each area. That is, a local worker is *more* fruitful at home, if time is pruned and cut by demanding service elsewhere. Conversely, a man might be made more fruitful in his far-flung outreach if he also adds a bit of respectful ministry to his local home base.
>
> Does this not fit your situation? Should we not make new believers and new churches feel that a very basic task is to reach out to other areas even before home base work has jelled? In fact, the reason why many a local church is like watery gelatin is because they sought to get it all together first, thinking they could later reach out more systematically. A very basic essential in establishing the local work is to reach out from its very inception. Born to evangelize. We establish ourselves by establishing others. We are seeing this principle in operation here. Our new outreach church has been a great thing for us, but it has cost.
>
> Always there is the feeling of burden with any new outgrowth, but this will be lessened if correct principles are applied. Amen!

Appendix 14

Testing One's View of the Church

Here in figure 8 I have diagrammed 1 Thessalonians 5:11-14. The blocks indicate those persons likely found in an average church. Ministries, or spiritual functions, mentioned in this text appear in the arrows indicating the one who performs or receives the ministry.

Figure 8: Diagram of 1 Thessalonians 5:11-14

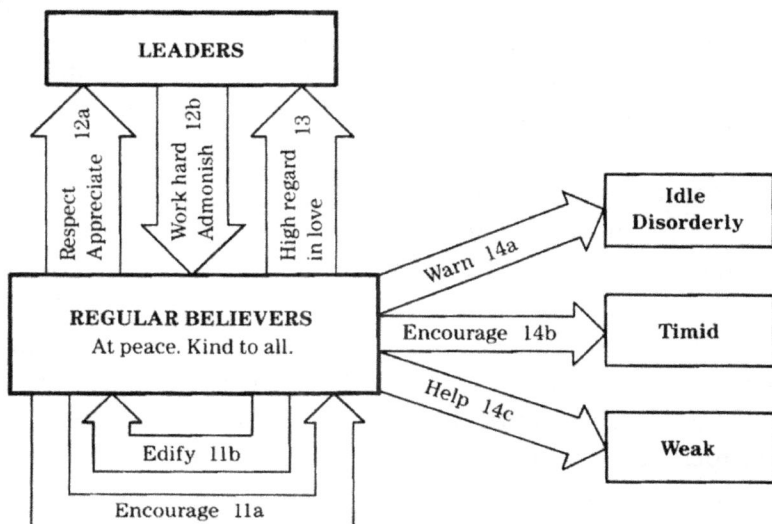

Appendix 15

My Personal Testimony, Written to Missionary Friends Abroad

Now, I want to give you a testimony of God's work in my own case. With the passing of time, things have changed with me. My goals in "church work" are different; my methodologies—or program ideas—have greatly altered. By His grace, I myself am not what I was. As servants of Christ, we cannot escape it: God never called us to "fill" a position—in the way we think of "filling the pulpit," or the like. "For this is the will of God, even your sanctification." "For God hath . . . called us . . . unto holiness" (1 Thess. 4:3, 7). Our *first* concern MUST be to BE what He wants; and once we get on with that, it turns out to be oh so different from what we expected!

Next, I am seeking to lead others along this same track. I am not THE minister. We are together servants of Christ—members of this one local body. Who knows what good "gift" will be bestowed? Where are old Bible elders and ministers, in the New Testament sense, *produced* by the church? My feeling is that a church can do far more than run a program, operate a budget, and then hire a professional "minister" to do its "ministering." What folly that we expect *you* (missionaries) to produce an indigenous church in that culture, from scratch, and we look to the seminaries and our all-sufficient budgets and thus "import" our "staff."

What a giant is the local assembly when filled by the Spirit! I feel like one commissioned to massage the sleeping members into a vital experience. This new life means a new love. I discover more homes are being opened as hearts are opened. (Christians need each other. Preachers do not have all the gifts.) We must cry to God to bring us up to the young church in Rome. They were "full of goodness, filled with all knowledge, able also to admonish one another" (Rom. 15:14).

The typical minister's life of pushing a rat-race schedule of programming and then toppling into a grave 'neath trees with abundant foliage and little fruit—this scares me. The years are already slipping by, so I want the Lord's help, and your prayers, as I get on with this boot camp. (The swatting of flies far behind the enemy lines makes good references for the next larger church but does not disturb the Enemy!)

What it would mean if we could present Christ with a new "body" here—into which new converts could be saved! There would be no more of that strolling "forward" to lightly "accept Jesus." The man who gets hold of a wire that is charged will pulsate with it. Frankly, I have begun to suspect that any good salesman could contract folks enough to fill up the empty seats, and maybe even get up his quota of "decisions." But, a church full of "decided" folks who hold the same Bible views and make the same choices of public entertainment *is still not a church*.

Besides these things, here is a summary list of important understandings and attitudes that have been growing lately within my heart—and I trust within others:

1. The sinfulness of sin.
2. The sufficiency of Christ and what it means to be in our Head. (Rom. 6–8; 1 Cor. 1:30; Ephesians).
3. Absolute necessity for personal holiness. To both practice

sin and profess Christ is impossible. Breaking with sin is a must. Philippians 1:6 does not say that we will be saved *anyhow*. It says that those who are surely and securely God's will be led on toward perfection. The others are none of His; there are no exceptions.

4. Growing hunger for God.
5. Love and concern for one another.
6. New regard for Satan, who powerfully thwarts us on every hand, unless the armor be complete and prayer constant.
7. Like babies learning to talk, we are now trying to pray—really pray. And faith appears like a first evening star—not too clear as yet, but with good prospects.
8. Some of our Savior's compassion for the multitudes of sheep without a shepherd.

It has taken too many years to get this little way. Jane and I are therefore asking God to help us teach our children all this. They need to know that there is no other *Christian* life, except that which gets on with the matter of holiness and abandonment to God. A life that *intends* to be less than perfect is that of a rebel, not a son. (Incidentally, I no longer give the old invitation: "How many of you Christian young people would be willing to do this or that if the Lord should call you?" The first thing is repentance—or perish (Luke 13:3), and one who has truly repented will not willingly resist His will (Heb. 10:26). A new convert does not have much light, but he is responsible to submit to that which he has and be just as perfect as God has called him to be. By our faulty preaching of repentance, faith, and security, we have oiled the tracks of backsliding and cushioned the place of sin. We need to help folks raise their guard against the flesh, Satan, and the world—deadly enemies.

My heart is full, and may the Holy Spirit minister abundantly to you as well.

—Harold E. Burchett

Appendix 16

Praying Effectively for One's Church

If you would pray for your own church, with results following, consider these prerequisites:

1. Having the mind of Christ toward the church
2. Understanding what a church is—as God sees and says it
3. Relating all Christian activity to the church.

Let's quickly take these in order, bringing a summary of the book into the dominion of prayer.

Having the Mind of Christ toward the Church
"Christ loved the church and gave himself up for her" (Eph. 5:25). This must be our attitude. Revelation 1 shows the Lord standing among the churches. Despite their faults, his concern is obvious. He seeks to restore and elevate them.

Christ therefore loves, even honors, his churches. Surely we must not do less.

Understanding What a Church Is
All believers form the church, and the church is made up of churches. Each of these churches bears some likeness to the whole, and Christ presides as its Head.

A varied gathering of believers may be said to be a part of

a church or churches but is not a church. See Matthew 18:15-20, where our Lord clearly distinguishes between the several believers and the church. Even though he promises, "I am in their midst," the small group is responsible to report "to the church." A church, then, weak though it may be, must have a degree of biblical structure—a body of believers led by leaders who fulfill the offices prescribed in Scripture. There is room for variety but no room for rejection of God's plan.

Relating All Christian Activity to the Church

The proper function of missionary activity is to establish the church. This is a large order. For who shall have the authority to say, "Here in this locality shall be an implantation of the Body of Christ"? None dare say that without divine credentials and direct authorization!

Ideally, outreach efforts should be viewed as issuing from the churches. Even where this is not possible, the ideal should be acknowledged. Assisting agencies should be viewed as a means of helping churches accomplish what God assigns in Scripture.

Prayer for churches, then, is in reality prayer for the fountainhead of Christian activity. And the church is the grand goal as well.

How, Then, Shall I Pray?

First, ask God to qualify you as to the prerequisites just discussed. He wants that for you. If the Head still lives with his Body, be very respectful. If you see there the bride of Christ, then for his sake love her. If you see the Spirit's temple, then honor that congregation.

Second, begin very positively. Thank God for every good quality you see. Beg him for every good blessing that would please our Lord. Consider how much is promised God's people to make them adequate personally and effective corporately. Go over each aspect of church life, and pray with earnest longing that God will bring good to his people.

Third, approach the needs and failures by identifying with them. Make it your church and your burden and failure. Consider our Lord's example of efficient tenderness as he relieves and removes the flaws from his bride in Ephesians 5:25-27. The sins are there, with all the hindering traditions, but the real blockage is that the Husband lacks loving representatives who will pray and touch the wounds with his touch.

Index of Scriptures Cited

www.ingramcontent.com/pod-product-compliance
Lightning Source LLC
Chambersburg PA
CBHW071530040426
42452CB00008B/959